I KNOW
ABSOLUTELY
NOTHING
A B O U T ™
SKIING

I KNOW ABSOLUTELY NOTHING ABOUT™ SKIING

A New Skier's Guide to the
Sport's History, Equipment,
Apparel, Etiquette,
Safety, and Language

Steve Eubanks and Robert LaMarche

Rutledge Hill Press
Nashville, Tennessee

Published in Nashville, Tennessee, by Rutledge Hill Press, 211 Seventh Avenue North, Nashville, Tennessee 37219.

Distributed in Canada by H. B. Fenn & Company, Ltd., 34 Nixon Road, Bolton, Ontario, Canada L7E 1W2.

Distributed in Australia by Millennium Books, 33 Maddox Street, Alexandria NSW 2015.

Distributed in New Zealand by Tandem Press, 2 Rugby Road, Birkenhead, Auckland 10.

Distributed in the United Kingdom by Verulam Publishing, Ltd., 152a Park Street Lane, Park Street, St. Albans, Hertfordshire AL2 2AU.

Typography by D&T Bailey Typesetting, Inc., Nashville, Tennessee

Inside illustrations by David Alden

Library of Congress Cataloging-in-Publication Data

Eubanks, Steve, 1962–
   I know absolutely nothing about skiing : a new skier's guide to the sport's history, equipment, apparel, etiquette, safety, and language / Steve Eubanks and Robert LaMarche : illustrations by David Alden.
      p.   cm.
   ISBN: 1-55853-440-7
   1. Skis and skiing.   I. LaMarche, Robert J.   II. Title.
GV854.E83   1996
796.93—dc20   96-32276
                                                              CIP

Printed in the United States of America

1 2 3 4 5 6 7 8 9—99 98 97 96

CONTENTS

ACKNOWLEDGMENTS

Successful books require the help and cooperation of countless people at every step of the writing and production process. We especially thank our editor, Mike Towle, and our publisher, Larry Stone, from Rutledge Hill Press, who have shown immeasurable faith and confidence in the *I Know Absolutely Nothing about*™ book series. Their patience and professionalism are unequaled. We also extend our appreciation to illustrator David Alden, who once again has created wonderfully funny and memorable "notes," without which this book would be incomplete.

Solid, dependable research, of course, is the foundation of any book project. In this area, Stacy Gardner of the National Ski Areas Association provided valuable insight and data. We also thank Bob Carney of the New York Times Magazine Group for taking such a keen interest in our project.

Last, but certainly not least, we thank our families for their unconditional love and support in all that we do.

INTRODUCTION

Having grown up in the South, where snow was something I saw only on television and skiing meant being pulled behind a boat in the summer, I can personally attest that your first experience on snow-covered slopes will be one of the most exhilarating experiences of your life. No words can adequately describe the feeling you get when you turn off a chairlift and face the breathtaking beauty of a white ski slope falling away from the bluest sky imaginable. The typical reaction is that you're sorry you waited until adulthood to experience the excitement and wonder of the world's most popular winter sport.

Beyond this exhilaration, the sport's culture, people, and activities—both on and off the slopes—all combine to create an unforgettable experience. Unlike many other sports, skiing allows all skiers, even beginners, to have a great time the first day they step onto the hill. Why? Because you don't have to spend hours listening to instructors, nor do you have to be concerned with what anyone else thinks of your performance. You can ski as slow or as fast as you like while enjoying the challenges of learning to master your new "slip-sliding" environment. The only pressure to succeed is that which you place upon yourself.

Whether you're sliding tentatively on snow for the first time, taking on the challenges of a more difficult run, trying out new skis, or just enjoying a relaxing afternoon in the outdoors, skiing offers an incredible world of adventure. This book has been written for first-time ski adventurers. If you are anxious about all the things, good and bad, that you've heard about the sport, this is a guide that will put you at rest with easy-to-digest information. It doesn't focus on technique—that's best left to a certified instructor on a ski slope—but rather on the essential information that will help get you started in the sport with a minimum of frustration and embarrassment.

Like all of the *I Know Absolutely Nothing*™ books, this story walks you through basics in a fun, fictional format. By following the exploits of a main character who shares your anxiety (and harbors similar dreams of adventure) as he searches for information on skiing, you'll learn where to go, what to wear, how to act, what to ask, and when to ask it. This is information you won't find in a travel guide, and it's presented in a way you won't find anywhere else in the bookstore. You'll also notice throughout the text a number of key terms typed in small caps, denoting early reference of key terms also explained in the glossary of chapter 11.

Granted, people in the ski business are very friendly and you'll most likely be treated with the utmost courtesy and respect by everyone you encounter while learning the sport, but don't expect the kind of sycophantic service our main character receives. That's why we wrote the book. You don't need to spend the day traveling to ski shops, calling every skier you know, or even surfing the net to learn the basics. Simply take a deep breath, turn the page, and plunge into a world of natural beauty, dynamic motion, and adrenaline rushes. Welcome to the world of skiing.

—*Steve Eubanks*

I KNOW
ABSOLUTELY
NOTHING
A B O U T ™
SKIING

ONE

A DOWNHILL DAY

Larry is in love with Jennifer. He sits at their regular table in their favorite lunch-time cafe, staring at his coffee and pondering the decision he has just made. He has decided he is going to propose marriage, and while his stomach churns at the prospects of being a married man, the alternative to marrying Jennifer is to not marry her, and that is unthinkable. He swirls his coffee and gazes at the landscape print on the wall beside him, knowing that sometime in the near future he is going to pop the big question.

Jennifer is late, but Larry's not surprised or angry. He can't recall the last time he was angry with her. He is, however, a little anxious. She sounded different when she called him. It wasn't a bad kind of different, just hesitant...or, maybe, excited...he couldn't tell which. His appetite dwindles with every passing minute. There's no way she knows of his intentions to propose. He hasn't told anyone, not even his roommate. Whatever is on Jennifer's mind, Larry knows this is not going to be an ordinary lunch.

"Hey, I'm sorry I'm late."

Startled, Larry turns to see Jennifer's smiling face. She touches his shoulder, bends down, and plants a kiss on his cheek. She then sits in the chair across from him.

"So, have you ordered?"

"No," Larry answers, still trying to snap out of his daydreaming state. "I was waiting on you."

"You're so sweet. You could have ordered for me. You know what I want."

"I know. I just got some coffee."

There's a brief, uncomfortable silence, and he decides to break it.

"So, what's up? You sounded different this morning."

"Oh, nothing. I just planned a trip without telling you. I hope you don't mind."

"A trip?"

"Yeah. A group from the office is putting together a ski trip, and to get the best deal they needed two more people. It's a great bargain. I brought the brochure."

She reaches for her briefcase, but he stops her.

"Whoa, whoa, whoa. Skiing? You mean, like, snow and mountains and all that stuff?"

"That's right," she says.

"Sweetheart, I know absolutely nothing about skiing. You know where I grew up. A sand dune on the beach is the closest thing to a mountain I've ever seen. I don't even know enough to be ignorant."

"Oh, it's easy. You'll love it. Cold, crisp wind whistling past you as you carve turns, float through POWDER, dodge moguls—"

"Dodge what?" Larry interrupts in something of a state of shock.

"MOGULS; you know, mounds of snow."

He doesn't know, nor does he understand, how she could think a warm-blooded southern beach boy would even consider letting cold wind whistle anywhere near him.

"Sweetheart, I can't go on a ski trip. I mean, cold wind, 'CARVING turns.' I don't even carve turkey."

"But you have to go, Larry. I've already signed us up."

"Well, unsign us."

She looks down at the table, and her mouth forms one of the prettiest pouts he's ever seen.

"The whole office is going. If we don't go, they won't get the good travel deal. They're counting on us." She turns away and stares out the window.

All the anxiety Larry felt just before Jennifer's arrival now lodges in his throat. He couldn't care less about her coworkers, but there's no way he can disappoint her. Cold or no cold, this is the woman he wants to marry. A few days on a snow-covered mountain won't kill him. At least, he doesn't think they will. He's heard plenty of stories about broken legs and dislocated knees, but rarely has he heard of anyone dying on the slopes. Of course, with his luck, he could end up being part of that unfortunate breed.

"I'm sorry, sweetheart," Larry relents. "I'll go. I won't promise I'll ski, but I'll go."

Her beaming smile warms the room. "You're going to love it, Larry. I promise you'll have a great time."

"I'm sure I will," he sighs, rolling his eyes.

Larry forces down his lunch while Jennifer continues to chat about EDGING, POLING, and countless other strange actions that to Larry spell instant death and mutilation. Maybe he'll be killed quickly so he won't freeze alone on a white mountaintop.

At the end of the hour, Jennifer kisses him good-bye, professes her love, and once again assures him that he's going to have a great time.

"Besides," she adds, "it's not until next month. You've got plenty of time to learn."

"Oh, sure," he mutters.

"Don't worry, you'll be skiing like Alberto Tomba before you know it. We'll have to pull you off the mountain."

"That's what I'm afraid of," Larry admits.

Jennifer laughs and heads back to work. Larry finishes his coffee and wonders what he has gotten himself into.

While driving back to the office, Larry notices a sign he must have passed at least a hundred times. It's for a shop called Ski Masters, which touts itself as Your Winter Sports Equipment Headquarters.

Larry whips his car into the parking lot and enters the store. Out of the corner of his eye, he catches a glimpse of an outdoor thermometer at a nearby bank, announcing in yellow neon a balmy sixty-six degrees. This certainly is not the kind of winter weather he's likely to face on this little junket he's gotten himself into, but then, how tough can this sport be? He still sees himself as a decent athlete, and he refuses to let his fear get the best of him. He can do this.

Larry enters Ski Masters with what confidence he can muster. The first thing he notices is a line of long, pointed skis stacked like spears against a wall. Above the skis hang several posters of men and women, airborne and in crouched positions, with a fleeting landscape dropping at an almost vertical angle beneath them. They're all dressed in colorful suits, and they all flash dazzling smiles, their teeth as white as the snow beneath them.

Seeing the photos only adds to Larry's anxiety. He is picturing himself launching off a mountaintop with missiles strapped to his feet when a handsome, athletic man in his early twenties approaches and asks, "May I help you?" The look on the young man's face shows that Larry's answer surprises him.

"I know absolutely nothing about skiing," Larry announces forthrightly. "I mean, I know nothing. I've never been, I've never watched it, I've never talked about it, and, as far as I can recall, I've never thought about it. This wouldn't be a problem, but my...(he starts to say fiancée)...girlfriend has booked us on a trip next month. I don't mind telling you I'm scared to death."

This brings a chuckle from the young clerk. "Don't worry. It's not as bad as you think."

Larry wonders how bad that might be. "Can anybody here help me?" he asks.

"You've come to the right place," the clerk declares. "Our owner is a former Olympic ALPINE ski racer. He still coaches, and he's also a consultant for an equipment company."

Larry raises his eyebrows and doesn't ask the first question that pops into his head, *What is a guy like that doing in a city where it's sixty-six degrees in the winter?* Instead, he broaches a more pressing issue. "So, do you think he has time to help me?"

The clerk retreats to the back of the store and returns in less than a minute with an older, taller, and even more athletic-looking man with graying temples and a strong, weathered face. Something about the man gives Larry the feeling he's in for an interesting downhill day.

Two

The Ski Story

"Hi, I'm Phil Mare," the distinguished-looking man says, extending his hand to meet Larry's. "Tommy tells me you have a little problem."

"That's a mild understatement," Larry replies. "I know absolutely nothing about skiing, and my girl-friend has booked us on a trip next month. Normally, I just wouldn't go, but her entire office is going, and, well, it's just that I don't want to embarrass her or myself."

Phil smiles, and Larry notes the man's chiseled features.

"Well, as long as you're willing to learn, you don't really have much to worry about," Phil declares.

"That's what *you* think. I know nothing. I mean, really, nothing."

"Don't worry," Phil chuckles. "You don't have to be young or athletic, or even coordinated, to enjoy skiing. What you do need is an understanding of a few fundamentals, and you need to be prepared to take on a winter mountain environment. I take it this is an Alpine ski trip?"

"A what?" Larry asks.

"An Alpine trip. You're downhill skiing, not CROSS-COUNTRY SKIING," Phil explains.

"See, that's what I mean," Larry declares. "I don't know the difference. I didn't even know there was more than one way to ski."

Phil puts a hand on Larry's shoulder. "Why don't you come back to my office. We'll take this one step at a time."

"Good idea."

The two walk to Phil's small but neat office where photos of snow-covered peaks adorn the walls. Larry is awed by the sheer vertical drops in some of the photos and the fact that people actually appear to be enjoying themselves as they plunge off cliffs. "Wow!" he exclaims as he stares at one of the photos.

"Yeah," Phil acknowledges, "that jump's all you want, even on a good day."

"You mean that's you?" Larry asks, looking back at the photo and the airborne figure flying off the edge of the earth with planks on his feet.

"Sure is. But that was several years ago. I haven't tried that run since I moved here."

"Wow!" Larry pronounces again, lacking anything else to say. "I guess I've come to the right place."

They both sit down, and Larry does his best to answer Phil's earlier question. "I guess we are doing that downhill thing...what did you call it?"

"ALPINE SKIING," Phil answers. "It's commonly referred to as downhill, and because it's the most popular form of skiing, most people just assume it's what you're talking about when you discuss skiing."

"But are there other kinds of skiing?" Larry asks.

"Actually, there are several, depending on how you categorize the sport. The two most commonly referred types are NORDIC, or cross-country skiing, and Alpine, or downhill skiing."

Larry takes out a notepad he brought and starts writing, knowing he probably won't be able to re-member, without notes, all the information about to come his way. "I take it these are what their names imply, down-a-hill or across-a-country," he com-ments.

"That's pretty accurate," Phil agrees. "Nordic, or cross-country skiing, comes from the Scandinavian countries where people first used skis as a means of traversing flat, open landscapes. It's one of the earli-est-known means of transportation."

"What possessed that first person to put boards on his feet?" Larry wonders aloud. "It's sort of like the first guy to eat an oyster. What was he thinking?"

Phil laughs. "Well, skiing definitely didn't start out as the sport we think of today. It was a means of getting around in the snow. In fact, archaeologists have recovered skis estimated to be forty-five hun-dred years old, so we know that the first skier lived a long time ago."

"I'm trying to imagine what he thought when he got to that first big hill," Larry muses.

"For the most part, the terrain in Sweden and Norway is relatively open and flat, and that's where skiing began. But when the Norwegians started migrating, skiing migrated with them."

"Viking skiers," Larry murmurs as he continues to take notes. "So, when did somebody decide you could actually make a sport out of skiing?"

"There's no real historical record of the first ski race, although it probably took place when some hunters decided to race while out on some trail somewhere."

"Last one to the elk herd is a rotten egg?" Larry jokes.

"Maybe. Nobody knows for sure. We do know, however, that in 1733 a fellow named Jens Henrick Emahusen wrote the first set of skiing rules for the Norwegian ski troops, so the sport of skiing can definitely be traced that far back. By the 1860s skiing had been established with a set of rules, and ski clubs sprouted all over Norway. Nordic skiing still has a large base of popularity. It's like combining a winter nature hike with an aerobic workout. It's great fun."

Larry glances up from his notes at the photo of Phil plunging off the cliff. "So, when did somebody finally decide to go down a mountain on those things?" he inquires.

"Alpine skiing didn't start until much later. Remember, to get down a mountain you first have to get up it, and that's no easy feat on skis. In 1897 Wilhelm Paulcke, a German, put together what he called

HOW ALPINE/DOWNHILL SKIING STARTED (MAYBE)

FIRST KNOWN RULES OF SKIING WERE WRITTEN IN 1733.

SKIING CAN BE TRACED BACK 4,500 YEARS.

ALPINE SKIING BECAME POPULAR IN THE LATE 1800s.

THE FIRST NORDIC CROSS-COUNTRY SKIER.

SKIING WAS FIRST USED AS TRANSPORTATION.

a SKI ALPINING, or SKI MOUNTAINEERING, tour of the Alps. For those skiers the climb was as important as the DESCENT. Heated GONDOLAS weren't around yet, although I'm sure a few of those mountaineers had some great ideas for improving the ascent."

"Heated what?" Larry asks.

"Don't worry, we'll get to that later," Phil assures him. "Anyway, those are the two main categories of skiing, and that's a brief history of how each started. There's even a hybrid form of the sport called TELE-MARK SKIING that has a rich past. In telemarking, skiers use a cross between cross-country and downhill skis to travel downhill. Like Nordic BINDINGS, tele-mark bindings allow the skier's heels to lift off the ski during turns. We'll talk more about bindings later."

Larry tells Phil that he remembers watching the last Winter Olympics on television and noticing that there seemed to be quite a variety of skiing events.

"Absolutely," Phil states. "For example, Nordic skiing has traditional cross-country racing and the BIATHLON. The latter tests the skills of cross-country racing and expert shooting. Alpine skiing is also rich in COMPETITION, with events such as:

- SLALOM,
- GIANT SLALOM and SUPER-G,
- DOWNHILL,
- COMBINED,
- MOGULS,
- BALLET,
- AERIALS, and
- JUMPS, although, technically, a Nordic event.

TYPES OF SKIING EVENTS

ALPINE
- SLALOM
- GIANT SLALOM
- SUPER-G
- DOWNHILL
- COMBINED

MOGULS

BALLET

AERIALS
- JUMPING

"All these events require different skiing styles, techniques, and strategies," Phil says.

"Hold it. Jumps?" Larry asks. "You mean, like, flying?"

"Yes. Jumping, now called SKI FLYING, is one of the oldest forms of competitive skiing. Skiers descend from a ramp and sail off a launch. The object is to fly, or stay in the air, as long as possible and to travel as far as possible. It is officially a Nordic sport, but many people confuse it with Alpine skiing because of the downhill elements. Anyway, it's one of the most exciting spectator sports."

"Oh yeah, I remember the old 'agony of defeat' footage that used to kick off ABC's *Wide World of Sports*," Larry agrees.

Phil laughs again. "You think *that's* bad? You should see some of the wipeouts that occur in FREESTYLE-aerial competition."

"I give up. What's that?"

"Freestyle aerials are some of the most spectacular midair acrobatics you've ever seen. Skiers gain speed going downhill, soar off steep snow ramps, and then perform flips, back-flips, and double-flips with half-twists. They're truly amazing to watch."

"Sounds dangerous," Larry declares.

"It is, and the competition is strictly regulated. But when done right, freestyle aerials are an art form."

Larry notes this, especially the double-flip with a half-twist part. He won't be trying that stunt regardless of what Jennifer says.

"What are those other types you mentioned? You said 'moguls.' Those are mounds, right?" Larry is proud of this little contribution, which he learned in his discussion earlier with Jennifer.

"That's right," Phil says. "Mogul actually comes from a colloquialism used in the Alps, *mugel*, which means 'small hill.' Usually, moguls are UNGROOMED areas on a slope where high ski traffic and snowdrifts form bumps. From the base of the mountain, moguls look small, but when you're skiing them, they often look pretty intimidating, even frightening. They can be treacherous, but they can also be a lot of fun."

Larry makes a note to steer clear of moguls.

"Anyway," Phil continues, "about the other types of skiing…"

Phil tells Larry about the various downhill events skiers enjoy. From the freestyle beauty of ballet to the excitement of downhill racing, Larry learns that skiing events are varied.

"You mentioned something called SLALOM," Larry says.

"Yes, slalom is a kind of racing where the skier makes a number of turns through tightly spaced GATES set up on the mountain."

"Gates? You mean like fences?"

"No. Slalom gates are pairs of poles that are placed in the snow to create a slalom racecourse. Skiers must make their way through the gates as quickly and accurately as they can."

"It sounds sort of like one of the drills my basketball coach used to make us do," Larry comments. "He

AERIALS

- FREESTYLE AERIALS ARE LIKE AEROBATICS ON SKIS

- GREAT TO WATCH

- DANGEROUS TO TRY

would set up chairs on the court and have us dribble through and around them as quickly as possible."

"That's a great comparison, but when you miss a gate on a racecourse, there's no going back," Phil points out.

"Duly noted," Larry states as he writes.

"Now, slalom racing also has a couple of variations—"

"Oh no," Larry interrupts, getting his pen ready.

"Don't worry," Phil says reassuringly. "It's nothing radical. As I've already mentioned, you have what's called the slalom, where the gates are fairly close together, putting a premium on accuracy instead of speed. Usually, skiers don't exceed forty miles per hour in a slalom competition."

Larry can't imagine ever exceeding forty miles per hour, period.

Phil continues, "The other kind of slalom races are called GIANT SLALOM and SUPER-G. In these, the gates are farther apart and the skiers combine greater speed with precise turning. But the most exciting races to watch are DOWNHILL events. Downhill racers reach speeds of seventy miles per hour while skiing down a course of very loosely spaced gates. Finally, there's a fifth Alpine competition known as the COMBINED, in which slalom and downhill times for individual racers are added together. The top competitors in the combined obviously possess diverse ski-racing talents."

Larry hopes he doesn't accidentally end up on one of those downhill courses. He then asks, "Who administers all these different events? I mean, is there a governing body in skiing that sets the rules?"

"Good question," Phil says, as he leans over and pats Larry's shoulder. "Yes, there is a ruling body of skiing. It's called the F.I.S., which stands for FEDER-ATION INTERNATIONALE DE SKI. It was formed in 1924 as the official governing body of ski competitions worldwide. But many ski clubs organize their own events. If you want to race your friend down a mountain, the only things stopping you are the rules of the particular ski area and, hopefully, your own common sense."

"Gee, thanks," Larry grunts. He gets a bad visual image thinking about racing anyone down anything where snow is involved.

"Since we're on the subject of racing, I should mention a few of the outstanding racers who have made the sport what it is today," Phil continues.

Larry readies his pen, and Phil looks thought-fully at the ceiling for a moment before proceeding.

"It's really hard to say who the best skier of all time would be," he begins. "The sport has changed so much through the years. But any discussion of great skiers always includes one man: Jean-Claude Killy."

"I take it he's French," Larry remarks.

"Yes, he is," Phil says, "and as far as all-time greats are concerned, Jean-Claude Killy is on every-one's list. He dominated the sport in the 1960s, and he is one of only two triple-gold-medal winners in

skiing in a single Winter Olympics. In 1968 he took
Olympic gold in every Alpine event—at the time,
slalom, giant slalom, and downhill—a feat that has
never been equaled."

"Wow!" Larry exclaims. Maybe he knows nothing about skiing, but he can certainly appreciate the
magnitude of winning three gold medals. "Who else
would you consider on the all-time A team?"

"In the 1950s a man named Toni Sailer of Austria was one of the most dominating skiers, although
Stein Eriksen from Norway was no slouch. Eriksen
won Norway's first Olympic gold medal in the giant
slalom in 1952. He also won a silver medal in the
slalom that same year. I guess he would be on the
A team. So would Pepi Stiegler from Austria, who
won gold, silver, and bronze medals in the 1960s;
Egon Zimmerman, who won downhill gold in
1964; Bernhard Russi from Switzerland, who won
downhill gold in 1972 and silver in 1976; and Sweden's Ingemar Stenmark, who won two gold medals
in 1980 and was a three-time World Cup champion.
Today you have greats such as Alberto Tomba from
Italy, and many others."

Larry immediately recalls the lunch meeting
with Jennifer and her reference to that Tomba fellow. At the time Larry had been too shocked and
embarrassed to ask who Tomba was. He jots down
more notes. "So, how about women? Are there any
famous women skiers?"

"Oh yes," Phil says. "Rosi Mittermaier from
Germany, and Americans Barbara Cochran, Tamara

McKinney, Donna Weinbrecht, Suzy Chaffee...the list goes on. Ski history is full of great drama provided by both men and women. If you're interested, you should look into some books and videos on past Olympics."

Larry makes a note to check the library and video store after he learns a little more about the sport. Of course, he won't be racing in the Olympics or in anything else for a while, so for now, he decides he needs to stick to the basics. "Okay, Phil, now that I know all the things I won't be doing for a while, where do we go from here?"

"The first thing we have to do is get you into a pair of boots and onto a pair of skis," Phil pronounces.

Larry stands and takes a deep breath. "I was afraid you were going to say something like that."

THREE

WEAPONS OF CHOICE

Larry follows Phil back into the store, where several customers are browsing through rows of skis and accessories. Phil motions his younger assistant over. "Tommy, I need to help some of these other people. How 'bout teaching our student some basics on equipment."

"Sure," the young man responds.

As he walks over, Larry takes a closer look. This is no kid. Tommy has the broad shoulders and trim build of an all-star athlete, and his bronze complexion gives depth to his youthful face. Tommy extends his hand, and Larry is surprised by the firmness of his grip.

"My name's Tommy Mole," he says. "I'm sorry I didn't formally introduce myself earlier."

"Tommy, I'm Larry. I hope you know what you've gotten yourself into."

Tommy laughs. "Hey, everybody was a BEGINNER once. So, do you know anything about ski equipment?"

"Absolutely nothing," Larry declares. "I know so little, you'll be stunned by how ignorant I am."

"Don't worry, it's not that hard," Tommy replies.

Larry isn't reassured. "Phil said something about boots and skis."

"Yeah," Tommy says. "Are you going to be Alpine skiing or cross-country skiing?"

"You know, Phil asked me that same question, and believe it or not, I didn't know there was a difference. That just tells you what a neophyte I am."

Tommy smiles and confides, "It's no problem. Look, everybody started some time. Someday this discussion will be ancient history, and, hopefully, you'll be an EXPERT skier."

"Wishful thinking," Larry demurs, returning his smile. "Anyway, we've determined this is an Alpine trip, but since you brought it up, do you need different stuff for cross-country skiing?"

"Definitely," Tommy says. "Cross-country skis are longer and designed with far less emphasis on turn features. You need to prepare yourself differently when you're cross-country skiing. What you wear, what you take—everything is a little different when you're cross-country skiing simply because you're covering different types of terrain."

"For the time being, let's stick to Alpine skiing," Larry declares.

"Okay, step over here," Tommy says, pointing to an area of the store where an array of large hard plastic boots hang from the wall. "We'll start with boots."

"You mean you actually *wear* these things?"

Tommy looks at Larry and grins. "Boots are the most important part of your equipment. They allow you to control your skis. Without the support they offer, you wouldn't be able to stand properly or control your movements."

Larry takes another glance at the assortment of colorful plastic boots. "I take it this isn't as easy as picking out a new pair of sneakers."

Tommy laughs again. "Don't worry. It's easy once you know the basics."

"Okay," Larry concedes, "what *are* the basics?"

Tommy takes down one of the large boots and hands it to Larry. "Ski boots have two main parts: the outer boot, or SHELL as it's sometimes called, which is made of hard plastic; and the INNER BOOT, which is firm but padded and normally made of insulating foam that molds to the shape of the foot. It's what keeps them dry and warm."

"It looks like something the Apollo astronauts wore," Larry remarks.

Tommy nods. "Don't be intimidated by their looks," he says. "Back in the old days, ski boots were made of leather. Now they're high-tech equipment that provide amazing performance on snow."

Larry looks at the latches and knobs on the boot he's holding. "Do you need a secret decoder ring to get this thing open?"

"No," Tommy assures him. He reaches over and flips a couple of buckles. "What you're holding is called a REAR-ENTRY BOOT, because the hard plastic shell hinges at the heel, or spine."

Tommy demonstrates by pulling open the heel portion. "You put it on by sliding your foot into the inner boot from the rear."

Larry looks at the boot, its back now open like a mechanical jaw. "You slide your foot in here and the buckles lock you in place. Is that it?"

"That's exactly right," Tommy replies, before taking down another boot from the wall. "You'll notice that the boot you're holding isn't as tall or as rigid as this one."

Larry sees that the boot in his hands is, indeed, lower than Tommy's. Tommy explains that beginner boots are usually designed to be lower, lighter, and a little more flexible, while expert and racing boots are taller and more rigid to provide greater support, dynamic feel, and precise STEERING.

"Your boot has an overlapping seam in the front with a few more buckles," Larry comments.

"Yep," Tommy answers. "This is a FRONT-ENTRY BOOT, and there are also MID-ENTRY BOOTS. For many newcomers to the sport, finding front- and mid-entry boots that fit properly takes a little more time and research than finding a good rear-entry boot. Front- and mid-entry models are also harder to put on and take off, but they have the advantage of providing better support and steering sensitivity."

"Wait a second," Larry interjects, holding up his free hand. "Steering sensitivity?"

"Sorry, I got ahead of myself," Tommy admits. "The most important thing to remember about boots is that you need them to fit comfortably, yet snugly.

They need to conform to the shape of your feet precisely. Most boots have fit-adjustment features, but a good shop can take a few extra measures to guarantee a custom fit. Nothing drives beginning skiers away from the slopes faster than poorly fitted boots."

Larry looks at the boot with all the buckles. "I can't imagine anything this big and cumbersome fitting comfortably," he contends.

"Well, it's relative. Believe me, if you're out on the slopes in boots that don't fit properly, you'll wish you had taken more time to find the right pair for you."

"What do you look for?" Larry inquires.

Tommy goes on to explain several things to watch for:

- First, when the boot is buckled up, you should not be able to move your heel up and down. You should have enough room in the front, though, to wiggle your toes.
- The boot also needs to hinge forward where your ankle hinges forward. It doesn't do much good for the boot to hinge halfway up your shin.
- You should not be able to move your ankle from side to side. If you can feel gaps between the inner boot and your ankle, the boots are too loose and you'll find it very difficult to ski under control. If you can't feel any internal movement, you'll improve more rapidly and your feet will stay comfortable longer.
- You should also flex your shins forward in your boots to check for support and comfort. The boot's front cuff should flex only forward.

THE BOOT

PREHISTORIC BOOT

SOLE — FRONT ENTRY

INNER BOOT

THE MODERN BOOT

FRONT ENTRY

BUCKLES

HINGE — MID ENTRY

SOLE

LEVER ADJUSTER — REAR ENTRY

TIPS
-GET A TIGHT BUT COMFORTABLE FIT-
-SPEND TIME IN BOOTS-
-WALK AROUND IN YOUR BOOTS-
-BE ABLE TO WIGGLE YOUR TOES-
-YOUR HEEL SHOULD NOT MOVE-
-BE ABLE TO FLEX AT ANKLE-
- TRY ON BOOTS WITH SOCKS YOU WILL
WEAR WHEN YOU ARE SKIING-

If you can also flex it laterally, you won't be able to steer your skis efficiently. Remember, a boot will flex more easily in a ski shop where the temperature is set at seventy degrees than it will out on the freezing snow. If a boot feels too stiff in the shop, it will feel even stiffer on the hill.

Larry puts down his boot and feverishly takes notes. "I assume that as a beginner, I need a light-weight rear-entry boot—"

"You need one that's comfortable and support-ive," Tommy interrupts. "Check all the things I've just mentioned. Don't settle for the first pair of boots you try on. Also, don't take one leisurely stroll around the ski shop and decide a particular pair is right. Spend ten to fifteen minutes in each model you try. Pay attention to how the boots feel. Skiing is a different act from walking or running, and you don't buy street shoes or running shoes without some thoughtful consideration. Do the same with your ski boots."

"Good point," Larry remarks, still writing. "After I've decided on a pair of boots, what's next?"

"Next we have to find a pair of skis that fit you."

"Skis that fit?" Larry asks. He understands the need for properly fitted boots, but skis are skis—at least that's what he thinks.

"Oh, absolutely," Tommy assures him. "Proper ski selection depends on your ability level, weight, ag-gressiveness, the type of snow you're going to be skiing on, whether or not you're skiing moguls—"

"No moguls," Larry interrupts.

"That's good," Tommy says. "You might not know much, but at least you're not foolish."

Larry takes that as a compliment and gets his notepad and pen ready. "How do I know what skis fit me? Do I try them on?"

"Not exactly. To get skis that fit, you must first consider your ability level."

"That's easy—*no* ability," Larry emphasizes.

Tommy laughs, then continues, "All ski manufacturers make models suited for beginners. Generally, they're shorter and lighter to be more maneuverable on the snow, a big plus for a first-timer. They're also more flexible, which allows the skier to control them in basic turns without having to make any aggressive movements.

"You should also know that skis are measured in centimeters. People often refer to ski lengths with numbers such as 160, 170, 200, and so forth. In general, the longer the ski, the faster you'll go."

"I take that to mean that if I ever get to be an expert racer, I should get 300- or 400-centimeter skis?" Larry queries.

"Not exactly," Tommy explains. "You see, longer skis are faster, but they're also harder to turn, so there's a trade-off. You want to balance your need for speed with your need for control. Beginners should start with shorter skis, but short skis aren't just for beginners. Some freestyle and mogul skiers use short skis because they need precise control more than they need speed."

"Then I guess I need really short skis," Larry concedes.

"You need *shorter* skis," Tommy declares, "but you need skis that work for your weight and aggressiveness. A good basic guide is that, as a beginner, you should use skis that are as long as you are tall. If you are 175 centimeters tall—that's five feet, nine inches—you should start with skis that are 175 centimeters long.

"You can find out how long skis are by looking at a ski's side. The centimeter length is usually engraved there. When you become an intermediate, you'll probably benefit from skis that are ten to fifteen centimeters, or four to six inches, longer than you are tall. The extra length will help you make smoother turns at greater speeds."

"My goals are definitely modest," Larry admits.

"For your first time out, I recommend you get skis that are 175 to 180 centimeters long. That's a little shorter than your height, but you're reasonably thin and, as a beginner, it's better to err on the side of using a ski that's too short than one that is too long. If, for some reason, you gain or lose a great deal of weight, consider modifying your ski length. If you weigh more, try longer skis. If you weigh less, go shorter."

Tommy walks over to a rack where skis are displayed. He picks up a bright red ski and brings it to Larry. "Now the next thing you want to look for is the design of your ski," he declares.

"They all look long and skinny to me," Larry comments.

SIZING YOUR SKIS

BEGINNER

SKIS ARE MEASURED IN CENTIMETERS.

SHORTER SKIS ARE SLOWER AND EASIER TO TURN AND CONTROL.

LONGER SKIS ARE FASTER BUT HARDER TO TURN AND CONTROL.

SPEND TIME WITH AN EXPERT WHEN GETTING FITTED FOR SKIS.

INTERMEDIATE

THE LENGTH OF YOUR SKIS DEPENDS ON YOUR HEIGHT, WEIGHT, ABILITY, AGGRESSIVENESS, AND TYPE OF SKIING.

ADVANCED

"They are, but some are skinnier than others, just like some are longer than others. Also, the internal construction of a ski determines its on-snow behavior. There are skis designed for floating through powder; skis designed for holding an EDGE on steep, icy racecourses; skis designed for the quick reactions required in nasty MOGUL FIELDS; as well as skis suited for freestyle, slalom, super-G, and about anything else you can imagine."

"How about spastic? Do they have skis for that?"

"Can't say they do," Tommy chuckles, "but you might want to consider one of the new HOURGLASS designs."

Larry looks back at the skis and tries to imagine what could possibly be shaped like an hourglass. They all look like spears to him. "Okay, I give up. What's an hourglass design?"

"To understand, you need to know the different parts of a ski," Tommy replies, holding up a ski and pointing. "Imagine the ski divided into thirds:
- the forward third of the ski is called the FORE-BODY;
- the center third is called the WAIST; and
- the rear third is called the AFTERBODY, or TAIL.

"Now, if you look closely, you'll see that the waist of the ski is narrower than the forebody and the tail."

"Yeah, it looks tapered," Larry interjects.

"Exactly. An hourglass design simply magnifies that taper." Tommy then turns to the rack and picks out another ski. "Here the forebody and tail are a good deal wider than the waist, giving the ski an exaggerated hourglass look."

Larry continues to write, then looks up and asks, "Why is that good for beginners?"

"The hourglass design gives the not-so-great skier more control because the ski turns with less effort. The downside is a loss of speed and stability when they're running flat on the snow."

"I'm not sure I consider that a downside," Larry rebuts. He pauses a moment to study the differences between the conventional and hourglass skis. Then he sees something he hadn't noticed before.

"Why are they bowed in the middle?"

Tommy explains that all skis are bowed, and the bow is called the CAMBER. He places a ski on the hardwood floor, and it's obvious that the ski touches the floor only near its tail and TIP. The ski's waist is suspended above the floor. This camber evenly distributes the skier's weight along the ski.

"Combined with the ski's hourglass shape, or SIDECUT," Tommy continues, "the cambered waist is pressured down into the snow by the skier during a turn, resulting in a clean, carved arc."

Tommy also explains that the front end of the ski curves upward to allow it to glide over irregularities in the snow. This curved end is called the SHOVEL.

"This is getting complicated," Larry contends.

"Not really," Tommy assures him. "Most qualified ski shops have people who can help you pick the right skis. Of course, like anything else you buy,

SKI DIAGRAM

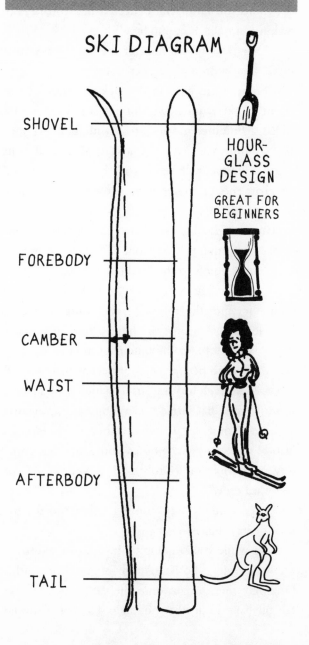

SHOVEL

HOUR-
GLASS
DESIGN

GREAT FOR
BEGINNERS

FOREBODY

CAMBER

WAIST

AFTERBODY

TAIL

the more you know, the better chance you have of making an intelligent purchase."

"Okay, let's take a look at the contraption that holds your boot in place," Larry suggests.

Tommy turns back to the rack and shows Larry a pair of skis with newly mounted BINDINGS. "It's called a binding, and it fastens your boot to your ski," Tommy says. "It's also a critical part of your safety equipment. It keeps your boot in place, and it's smart enough to know when to release your foot during a fall."

Larry stands a little straighter and pays close attention. Not hurting himself is one of his first priorities.

Tommy points to the binding's toe piece. "To attach your skis," he tells Larry, "you place the toe of your boot into the toe piece, then you press your heel downward against the hinged heel piece until your boot locks into the binding. On cross-country skis, there is no heel piece. Your heel actually lifts off the ski with each forward stride, which makes it easier to traverse flat surfaces. On Alpine skis, your toes and heels must stay firmly attached to the ski. It's critical that you put the boots in the bindings properly, otherwise you'll probably lose your skis at an awkward time."

"Like while you're coming down the mountain?" Larry suggests.

"Or while you're going up it," Tommy retorts. "I know one guy who hadn't fully engaged one of his bindings when he got onto the CHAIRLIFT. His ski fell off halfway up the mountain. He was lucky he didn't injure someone. Still, he was pretty embarrassed when he had to ask for a ride down the mountain on a snowmobile."

"Not good," Larry comments.

"Not good at all," Tommy echoes. "There are enough challenges on the mountain without creating more on your own, so make sure you have your bindings engaged. You should also have them regularly checked and adjusted."

The thought of crashing continues to trouble Larry. "How do I know if my bindings are adjusted properly?"

"You don't, and you shouldn't try to learn. Take them to an expert, a ski mechanic. Most ski shops keep someone on staff who can adjust your bindings according to your weight, the type of skis you're using, and your ability. If you can't get it done at a ski shop, be sure it's done at the ski area before you go out on your first run. Like I said, there are enough obstacles out there without creating new ones."

Larry writes away.

"Are you planning to rent or buy your equipment?" Tommy asks.

"I didn't know I had an option."

"You do. Almost every ski shop and ski area offers rental equipment. In fact, most beginners rent equipment, and even some experts decide renting is more convenient than lugging skis through airports."

Larry looks back at the long skis and sees Tommy's point. "What do I do if I want to rent equipment?" he asks.

"You want to look for several things," Tommy says before explaining further:

- First, make sure you know what you want before you walk into a rental shop. The level of service you get could depend on how busy the rental shop is and the experience level of the people working there. The more you know ahead of time, the better chance you have of getting what you want.

- The other problem you might have is the rental shop's inventory. If you know you want 175-centimeter hourglass skis and size-ten rear-entry boots, you might find that rental shops are out of what you need, particularly during busy holiday periods. It's sort of like renting a car for Christmas week. You might get what you want; then again, you might not.

- Also, remember that the equipment you rent is just that, rented. It's been used before, probably many times, and you need to check the quality and wear and tear of the gear. Check to make sure ski edges are sharp and free of rust. Look to see if the skis' BASES have been freshly waxed. Examine bindings for unusual wear, and double-check that they're securely mounted.

- The last thing to consider is transporting your equipment. Even if you rent your equipment from the ski area where you're staying, you still have to get it from one place to the next. How are you going to transport your skis? How are you going to carry your boots? Where and how are you going to store your skis? I know it sounds like a lot of things to consider, but the logistics of a ski trip can sometimes be more difficult than the skiing.

"This is incredibly complicated," Larry declares while writing. "Let's assume I figure out where I'm getting my skis and boots. I have the bindings checked, and I figure out how I'm going to get from point A to point B with all my stuff. Is that all I need?"

Tommy laughs. "Not quite. In terms of hardware, you still need POLES."

"Poles?" Larry questions with a puzzled look on his face.

"Poles," Tommy repeats. "Ever seen a tightrope walker?"

"On television."

"What do they always carry?"

"A balancing pole," Larry remembers.

"Right. And in skiing you have poles that help you start turns and propel yourself while you ski. Fortunately, poles aren't very complicated. They have handles and straps on one end, and BASKETS and POINTS on the other. You put your hands through the straps and grasp the poles so you don't have a total YARD SALE when you fall."

"A total *what?*"

Tommy laughs again. "A yard sale. That's ski slang for wiping out so badly you leave skis, poles, hat, camera, and everything else you carried strewn all over the mountain, just like a yard sale."

TAKE ONLY WHAT YOU NEED!

HOW TO GET FROM POINT A TO POINT B WITH ALL YOUR GEAR

CAREFULLY

- PLAN LOGISTICS.
- CONSIDER EQUIPMENT THAT CAN BE RENTED.
- BUY OR RENT CARRIERS FOR SKIS, POLES, AND BOOTS.
- CHECK OUT PARKING AND RESORT TRANSPORTATION.

"Very funny," Larry utters sarcastically while picturing his first yard sale. It isn't a pretty sight. "Do poles come in all shapes and sizes, or does one size fit all?"

"All shapes and sizes," Tommy says. "But don't get carried away. The way to size poles is simple. Hold the poles upside down at the base of the baskets while keeping your arms at the side of your body, with your hands about a foot in front of you. This approximates your standard arm-hand pole positioning when skiing. If your forearms and biceps form a ninety-degree angle, the poles are the right length. Don't worry about design. As a beginner, you just need to make sure your poles aren't bent or broken."

Larry writes down all the information about poles while Tommy speaks to another customer. After he finishes his notes, Larry glances around the ski shop and is surprised by something he thinks he recognizes. He turns back to Tommy.

"Hey, Tommy, do you guys sell surfboards here, too?"

Tommy laughs. "I guess you could say that. Come over here and I'll show you."

FOUR

SURFING THE SNOW

As Larry gets closer, he sees that the boards hanging on the wall are smaller than surfboards, and they have what look like half-boot bindings attached toward each end. It doesn't take Larry long to realize these are the skiboards. Having surfed most of his life, he gets an interesting visual image of how these things work.

"I take it these are skiboards?" Larry inquires.

"SNOWBOARDS," Tommy corrects.

"And," Larry continues, "I assume they're used for surfing on snow?"

Tommy nods. "I've never heard it put exactly like that, but you're right. In principle, SNOWBOARD-ING is like surfing on a ski slope, especially in deep powder. Interestingly, snowboarders have, until recently, shared the same sort of image problems surfers have suffered from for years."

"Hey, finally, something I can speak firsthand about!" Larry exclaims. "Where I grew up, if you owned a surfboard you were considered a brain-dead beach bum with no life. That stereotype used to drive me nuts."

"Yeah," Tommy concedes. "I snowboard and ski, and when I go out with my board, I'm looked at a lot differently than when I have my skis with me. The fact is, snowboarding is the fastest-growing outdoor winter sport. Twice as many people take up snowboarding as skiing every year, so the sport is quickly entering the mainstream. I think the image problem stems from the fact that, as a group, snowboarders are younger than skiers, and they tend to be a little less disciplined, more radical, and carefree about their sport."

Larry looks at one of the boards and sees the word *Apocalypse* across its back. "I guess the names are a little off the beaten path as well."

"Oh yes, that's a mild one. Snowboarders like their renegade image."

"Yeah, surfers do, too, even those who have steady jobs," Larry affirms.

Tommy takes down one of the boards. "A lot of people are trying snowboarding—some out of curiosity and some because they want the convenience of a snowboard. The biggest factor, though, is the cultlike following. Snowboarding is like a religion, and there are some pretty avid riders out there. They shred the mountains like food processors."

"Sounds charming."

"Oh, they love it. Snowboarders wear their cutting-edge reputations like badges. Even if they are accountants or lawyers, they join the radical masses as soon as they strap on their boards."

"Sounds more like surfing every minute," Larry declares. "What if I want to learn snowboarding? Is it like skiing?"

"Yes and no," Tommy responds. "It's like skiing in the sense that it requires balance, patience, and a good deal of practice to become proficient, but snowboarding's learning curve is quite a bit different from skiing."

Larry has his notepad ready. "What do you mean? How is it different?"

"Skiing is actually easier to learn initially; but once you reach a certain level, it takes a lot of work to move to the next level. It's a difficult sport to master. Snowboarding, on the other hand, is tougher to learn on the front end; but once you get it, you're riding. You can improve fairly quickly once you've mastered the fundamentals."

"Basically, you learn the two sports at different rates," Larry comments. "Again, it's much like surfing compared to, say, water skiing."

"I guess so," Tommy admits. "The big difference with skiing is that your feet face forward and your toes always point toward your ski tips. This alignment allows you to learn skiing with some basic beginner techniques, like SNOWPLOWING, that control speed and direction."

"Snow-what?"

"Snowplowing," Tommy repeats. "But don't worry, you'll learn that technique when you take

SNOWBOARDING IS LIKE SURFING ON THE SNOW.

IT'S HARD TO LEARN SNOWBOARDING,
BUT ONCE YOU LEARN, YOU BECOME
GOOD VERY QUICKLY.

SHREDDING THE MOUNTAIN

your first lesson. The point is, you can get proficient enough on skis to move around and go down slopes in a fairly short time, maybe a half-day.

"Snowboarding is different. Instead of facing directly forward, your feet are positioned at an extreme angle to one of the snowboard's edges. This means you have a blind spot on your back side. By the way, you should take this into account when you ski close to a snowboard rider. If his blind side is facing you, don't expect him to be able to make any moves to avoid you. Be cautious.

"The only way to turn and control a snowboard is to TILT it on edge and pressure it," Tommy continues. "That's tough for a beginner."

"But once you get up and going," Larry pursues, "it's a lot easier to learn snowboarding, right?"

"In general, yes," Tommy concedes. "I think one of the reasons for that is the improvement in snowboard design. Now they're precision, state-of-the-art instruments. This hasn't made it easier to learn the basics, but it has shortened the learning curve from beginner to expert."

Larry writes all this down and decides that if this whole snow thing turns out to be something he enjoys, he might pick up a board and take a walk on the wild side. Jennifer would love that. Just when she gets him away from the beach and out on the snow, he takes up surfing again!

FIVE

FULLY EQUIPPED

Another flurry of customers enters the store and Tommy's expression changes to one of mild concern.

"Tommy, thanks a lot," Larry says. "I think I know enough to make my first trip."

"Oh no," Tommy demurs. "We still have to get you outfitted. I need to help these other customers, but Pic can get you suited up and ready to go."

Larry wonders who or what a Pic is as he follows Tommy across the store. More customers arrive, and Tommy quickens the pace.

A young, attractive blonde woman with strikingly athletic features and an infectious smile finishes speaking with a customer at one corner of the store. Tommy calls to her. "Pic, I need your help."

The young woman walks over.

"Pic, this is Larry. He's sort of our student for the day," Tommy explains.

"I know absolutely nothing about skiing," Larry tells his newest acquaintance. "That wouldn't be a problem, but I'm going on a ski trip with a group next month."

The young woman's smile widens.

Tommy says to Pic, "I was hoping you could teach Larry a few things about apparel, what to take...you know, all the stuff he needs."

"My pleasure," Pic announces.

Tommy goes across the store to help other customers, and Larry follows Pic to an area filled with clothing and accessories. Larry is sure he misunderstood Tommy, so he asks the young woman to repeat her name.

"It's Picadilli. Picadilli Lane, but you can call me Pic."

"Your mother named you Picadilli?" Larry questions.

"I know, I know. My folks went to London just before I was born, so I ended up with a name I have to explain every day."

"Gee, pity they didn't visit Abbey Road," Larry says.

"I've said the same thing for years," Pic answers. "So, tell me what you've learned so far."

"Well, I know a little about the history of skiing and the different types of competitive events. I know enough about skis, boots, bindings, and poles to spend a lot of money, and I'm toying with the idea of snowboarding."

"Oh, a renegade. You're a man after my own heart," Pic responds. "We have to make sure you make the right fashion statement when you hit the slopes."

"I'm going to look goofy regardless of what I wear," Larry pronounces, thinking about the colorful suits worn by the skiers in the pictures. "I think making a fashion faux pas is the least of my worries."

Pic laughs. "Fashion is one thing; FROSTBITE is another. You need to learn a few basics about apparel just for your own safety."

Larry sighs and gets his notepad ready. "Okay, suit me up."

"The first thing to remember about skiing is to take nothing for granted," Pic declares. "A snow-covered mountain is the most hostile environment on the planet, more dangerous than the desert, the ocean, or the jungle. You have to prepare and dress accordingly."

Larry decides to cut the wisecracks. This is serious stuff.

Pic points to another photo of a skier in full attire. "Start by designing your wardrobe to fit the elements. Dress warmly, but also remember that skiing is an active sport. It requires a full range of body movements, so pick clothes that allow you to flex and stretch freely."

"You're going to have to help me," Larry pleads. "Right now, my vacation wardrobe consists of shorts and T-shirts."

"Okay," Pic agrees. "Ideally, you should dress in layers. Three layers should be sufficient to handle most winter conditions." She proceeds to explain the different layers:

- The purpose of the first layer—your undergarments—is to hold in your body heat, while moving, or WICKING, moisture away from the surface of your skin. Remember, no matter how cold it is, you're going to sweat. You need long undergarments that will transport sweat to outer layers of clothing. This will keep your skin dry and comfortable. Many skiers wear thermal cotton underwear, but it doesn't wick well, and it tends to be bulky. You might want to go high-tech—and spend a little more money—with an underlayer of polypropylene or one of the other new synthetic fibers specifically designed for its moisture-wicking properties.

- Your second layer is your absorbing layer. In addition to holding body heat in, it should absorb the moisture your first layer pushes out. This can be anything from a turtleneck to a wool sweater to some pretty sophisticated material blends, including synthetic fleece. You might be interested to know that some synthetic fleece is made from recycled plastic bottles. It's one of the ways skiers stay in tune with the environment.

- Your outer layer is critical, too. Its job is to keep moisture out. Remember, snow is wet. You want to stay dry. You need an outer layer that not only keeps you warm and keeps moisture out, but also breathes, letting perspiration evaporate. Of course, you can add layers as weather dictates, but be careful. It's easy to reach a point where your clothing restricts your movement, and that defeats the whole purpose of being on the slopes.

Larry writes away. "Okay, I'll buy some new long underwear, and I've got a couple of turtlenecks and sweaters. But I'm not sure about that last layer."

Pic nods and moves to an area of the store where colorful jackets, pants, and one-piece ski suits hang from display racks.

"You have several options when it comes to your outer layer," she explains. "Here's where you can be fashionable."

Larry spots another picture hanging nearby, this one showing a racer in full TUCK position, dressed in what appears to be a Spiderman outfit. "Is that what you mean by fashion?" he wants to know, pointing to the photo.

"Believe it or not, that was the U.S. Ski Team's uniform a few years ago," Pic answers. "Granted, that's not the fashion statement recreational skiers make, but the composition of that outfit is as technologically advanced as you'll find."

"What do you mean?" Larry asks.

"Well, I just explained that your clothing needs to keep you warm and dry while giving you a full range of motion, but in the past there was a big trade-off. Ski-wear insulation was thick and warm, but it severely restricted motion. Now, several new synthetic materials—such as Gore-Tex—keep jackets, pants, and ski suits lightweight and flexible. They allow body perspiration to evaporate but don't allow water to penetrate. Unfortunately, these materials are also expensive. Unless you ski regularly, the cost of this high-tech ski wear might be prohibitive."

Pic shows Larry a variety of ski pants in both stretch and quilted materials. She explains that with each there are trade-offs between warmth, flexibility, and price. She recommends that Larry select loose-fitting ski overalls, with a bib and suspenders.

Pic also shows him a variety of ski jackets and explains that the same principles apply. Versatility, breathability, warmth, and freedom-of-motion are highly desirable. She advises Larry to pick a jacket with enough pockets to accommodate a small camera, TRAIL MAPS, glasses, and other sundry items such as lip balm and sunscreen. She also warns him to check the zippers and linings for durability.

After looking at all his options, Larry chooses a red jacket that features a midpriced insulating material, zip-off sleeves, and four outside pockets. At Pic's insistence, the jacket is a full size larger than normal so he can wear several layers underneath and still move freely.

"Okay, this is a great start," she announces.

"Start! I thought we were finished."

"Oh no," Pic warns him. "You have your pants and jacket, but what do you plan to do about your hands and feet? And what about your head? How are you going to keep your ears and fingers from getting frostbite?"

Larry looks down, embarrassed.

"Don't worry," Pic reassures him. "It's a common mistake, even among more experienced skiers. You get up on the slopes, the temperature seems warm enough, and your adrenaline gets pumping. Before you know it, the temperature falls, you've left some area of your body unprotected, and you end up with a case of frostbite."

"I guess I need gloves and a hat," Larry concedes with a shrug.

"Always, always, always wear gloves and some form of a hat. Most of your body's heat is lost through your extremities, especially your head; so let's start there. The keys to headwear, again, are warmth and dryness. Safety is a consideration, too. There are, literally, hundreds of different ski caps to choose from, ranging from a simple knitted wool hat to a cap with a brim and insulated ear flaps.

"Also, I hate being the first to tell you, but you're going to fall more than once. You don't want to take any unnecessary risks, so you might want to consider wearing a helmet. A growing number of skiers are sporting helmets these days. They're lighter and warmer than ever before, and they even have eye-catching graphics. Helmet shells are also made of plastic, so moisture from snow or rain will never reach your head."

"Good idea," Larry declares. "Now, what about gloves?"

"Again, models that keep your hands warm and dry are important. You might even consider wearing two pairs of gloves together—a silk inner pair as an insulator and a larger outer pair to stay dry. A few manufacturers now make component glove systems that feature inner and outer gloves."

"Sort of like the layering of your other clothes?" Larry offers.

"Exactly," Pic acknowledges. "For an extra measure of dryness, you might consider a design like this." She lifts a glove off a shelf. "It has elastic at the wrist to seal out cold air and moisture, but it also has a loose shaft of material that's designed to overlap a few inches of your ski jacket sleeves. This also helps keep out loose snow, especially when you fall.

"For greater warmth, I'd recommend ski mittens instead of gloves. Because the four fingers are kept together in a mitten, body heat spreads and your hands stay warmer. The big advantage of gloves over mittens, though, is that you have greater dexterity with your fingers, making it easier to pick things up."

Larry writes, and Pic pauses to make sure he has it all down.

"Socks," she says after a moment.

"I'm sorry?" Larry, bewildered, inquires.

"Socks. You need socks."

"I have a drawer full," he states.

"Probably not what you need," Pic tells him. "To compensate for the cold weather, most people wear heavy socks—sometimes two pairs. But that's a mistake. Today's inner boots have foam that effectively insulates the feet. There are also several types of heaters that can be added to boots to provide extra warmth. These are great for skiers with poor circulation."

Pic goes on to explain that the main reason skiers shouldn't wear heavy socks is that the socks' softness and thickness create a delayed reaction when a skier applies pressure to his or her boot. This delayed response reduces control, creating a real safety problem. That's why socks specifically made for skiing are fairly thin, but they do provide some extra insulation against the cold. Ski socks are also tall enough to cover the calf so the boot won't press its top edge against the skin.

Pic selects a pair of socks from the rack and stretches them to demonstrate. She continues: "When you try on ski boots, wear the same socks you'll wear while skiing. If you try on boots while wearing a thick pair of athletic socks, you'll get a sloppy fit that will make skiing more difficult."

"Just like running," Larry notes. "If you wear two pairs of athletic socks when you run, you should always size your shoes wearing two pairs of athletic socks."

"Exactly," Pic affirms. "When you're sizing all your clothing and equipment, you want to simulate the conditions on the slopes as closely as you can. That means putting on all the layers. Only when you've put the whole ensemble together will you know what sizes are correct and whether or not you can move."

"I'm sure I'll fall just fine, regardless of what I'm wearing," Larry contends.

"You probably don't want to hear this, but you're right—you will. The more prepared you are for that eventuality the better."

Larry looks one more time at the picture of Spiderman racing at some incredible speed. "So really, why do people wear such bright colors? Is it like golfers' affinity for plaid?"

She laughs. "A lot of it is fashion, but a lot of it is safety. You want to be seen out there, not just by other skiers but by rescue teams in the event of an accident. Bright colors stand out against the snow. With that red jacket, people will be able to see you from a distance."

"Oh, that's great," Larry states. "I'm totally spastic, so I'll draw attention to myself by wearing bright red."

"Better than wearing something nobody will see," she replies.

"I guess so. Is there anything else I need?"

"Goggles," Pic says. "You might think this isn't important, but believe me, you can't ski if you can't see, and you can't see without a good pair of DUAL-LENS GOGGLES."

"Dual lens?"

"Yes. They work like storm windows," Pic remarks. "Dual lenses trap a layer of air between an inner and an outer lens to provide insulation and to reduce fogging. Also, make sure your goggles are ventilated and treated with defogging chemicals. If you've ever been inside a car on a cold morning, you know how quickly windows fog up. Your goggles can fog up just as quickly, and having your vision impaired while you're going down a mountain can be hazardous."

"Dual lens, antifog," Larry murmurs as he writes. "What else?"

"You definitely want sunscreen. If you think sand and water reflect the sun's rays, you should see what snow can do. One good day on a sunny slope, especially at high altitude, and your face could look like you had spent a week at the beach. A tube of lip balm is another must for skiers. It's critical to protect sensitive lips from cold, wind, and sun. Finally, you might want to consider a backpack, or FANNY PACK, if you plan to carry anything such as a video camera. You also need to consider how to transport your skis."

"I know, Tommy and I had that discussion."

"Let me just remind you then that skis are bulky, cumbersome things that can be a pain to carry any appreciable distance. You should consider buying lightweight bags for your skis, boots, and accessories. They're relatively inexpensive, and they can really save a lot of headaches."

After a few minutes of writing, Larry looks up and sees that his lesson must be over. Pic is smiling politely and looking past him toward other customers. "I guess that about does it," he declares.

"I don't know about that. You're outfitted, but you still have a few more things to learn," she counters.

Phil Mare has finished with his customers, and he rejoins Larry and Pic. "I heard that," he says. "Larry, I've called a friend of mine who owns a travel agency a few blocks away. If you have time, you should go by and talk with her. She's worked for ski resorts most of her life, and she books hundreds of ski trips a year. It would be helpful if you

LAYERS, LAYERS, LAYERS

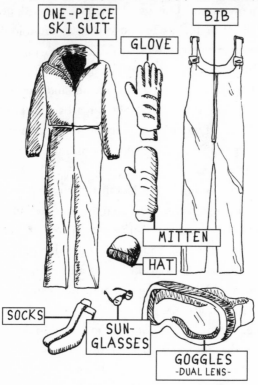

ONE-PIECE SKI SUIT

GLOVE

BIB

MITTEN

HAT

SOCKS

SUN-GLASSES

GOGGLES
-DUAL LENS-

ALWAYS WEAR
A HAT, GLOVES,
AND GOGGLES.

DRESS IN AT
LEAST 3 LAYERS.

BE WARM, BUT
BE ABLE
TO MOVE.

learned a little about what to expect before you show up at the slopes."

"You're right," Larry responds, as he accepts a note from Phil with the travel agent's name and address. "Phil, I can't thank you enough. I won't be an expert, but I won't be totally ignorant either."

Phil smiles and shakes his hand. "You're quite welcome, Larry. Good luck."

Six

Base Basics

Larry has no trouble finding the travel agent's office, but he has some trepidation about this next meeting. Although Phil called ahead, and the travel agent is expecting him, Larry has already bared his ignorance to enough people for one day. The thought of saying, "Hi, I'm Larry, and I'm a moron," is not appealing.

He takes a deep breath and opens the glass door that proudly displays the agency's logo. Before he can step fully inside, a tall woman with jet black hair and one of the widest smiles Larry has ever seen greets him with an outstretched hand.

"You must be Larry," she says, firmly shaking his hand.

"Yes, I am."

"I'm Tammy McKinley. Phil told me you were coming. I understand you know absolutely nothing about skiing."

"Well, I know a little more than nothing, now that I've visited Phil's store."

"Yeah, he's a great teacher. Too bad you couldn't take a ski lesson from him."

Larry nods and makes a mental note to ask about lessons.

"I know a few things about equipment and the different types of skiing," he says, "but I've never been to a ski area. As far as I'm concerned, I might as well be visiting a foreign country."

Tammy laughs. "Don't worry. You just need to learn a few basics that will make your first visit much easier."

"I'm all for easy," Larry confides.

"Are you going to be Alpine skiing or cross-country skiing?" Tammy asks.

"Alpine, but since you asked, where would *you* go to cross-country ski?"

"Anywhere that's flat and has snow," Tammy answers, smiling. "No, really, there are lots of areas designated for cross-country skiing, particularly in the Midwest. But check with your travel agent. If you want to dedicate a day of your trip to cross-country skiing, most ski areas have places where that's possible. Some all-season resorts have a golf course or another large recreational area that in the winter can be used as a cross-country ski course."

"That's clever," Larry comments.

"Ski resorts try to cater to everyone," Tammy acknowledges, as she walks over to her desk and points to a large world map hanging on the rear wall of the office. "Okay, we know you're Alpine skiing. Any idea where you're going?" she asks.

"To a mountain," Larry answers, realizing for the first time he has no idea what part of the planet he's about to visit. "I'm sorry, no. I just know we're Alpine skiing. I guess all mountains aren't alike."

"Oh my," Tammy comments, grabbing a pen to use as a pointer. "You're right. All mountains are not alike. As you can see from the dots on this map, it's possible to ski on almost every continent. In fact, some of the world's best ski areas are in places you wouldn't expect, such as Argentina and Australia."

Larry does his best to draw a world map in his notepad.

Tammy continues, "The one thing you can say about all these ski areas is that everywhere you go, the sport is a little different. You'll experience different types of snow, different elevations, and different cultures. You'll even find different things to do when you aren't on the slopes. Here in the United States, for example, the most popular resorts are in the Northeast and West, and each is very different. States such as Vermont, for instance, have large ski areas set around some of the most comfortable, traditional, and quaint New England villages you've ever seen.

"A New England ski trip is like vacationing inside a Norman Rockwell painting. Western resorts, such as those found in Colorado and Nevada, are vastly different. The towns and the people still reflect the rugged attitude of the Old West, and there's a certain freedom that you experience there that's different from anywhere else in the world."

SKIERS, SKIERS EVERYWHERE

Larry smiles and says, "Tammy, I'm not searching for my inner self or anything. I'm going on this trip because my girlfriend booked us."

She laughs. "I'm sorry I got carried away, but you never know—you might learn more out on those mountains than you think. Of course, those are just two examples. You can ski in Michigan, North Carolina, Pennsylvania, Arizona, New Mexico, and lots of other states. Each one offers a unique experience. If, after this first foray, you catch the ski bug, you can research resorts in a number of magazines and books. *Snow Country* magazine, for example, annually ranks the country's top ski resorts, based largely on reader input. The ratings allow you to compare the differences among ski areas."

"I don't know much, but since my passport has expired, I bet we're staying in this country," Larry says.

Tammy concurs, adding, "All ski areas are different, but there are a few similarities you can expect from most resorts you visit. And there are some basics you need to follow regardless of where you're going."

Larry readies his pen and pad.

"First, most resorts have a ski lodge at the foot of the mountain. It's often designed like a chalet, but that's not always the case. Many lodges have numerous distinctive architectural features."

Larry looks up from his notes. "I take it the lodge is where you rent your skis, right?"

"You can rent your skis in the lodge's ski shop," she answers. "You can also purchase most of the apparel and accessory items you need. The lodge is also where you sign up for lessons. Sometimes that's in the ski shop, and sometimes there's a separate area for lesson appointments. It really depends on the layout. Usually, though, lodges are very well marked."

"What about food?" Larry asks, envisioning himself stranded out in the snow with no means of nourishment.

"I can say with almost total certainty that the ski lodge you visit will have nice dining facilities with either a cafeteria-style, quick-service setup, or a sit-down-and-order area where you can probably look out at the mountain," Tammy replies, before pausing to allow Larry time to write.

"You're traveling with a group, right?"

"Right."

"Any idea how close your hotel is to the mountain?"

"No."

"I assume that you're going to try skiing a few mountains, depending on how many days you plan to stay?"

"Why do you say that?" Larry queries.

"You ski the mountains because they are there," Tammy says, then laughs at her own joke. "Seriously, regardless of where you're going, there are probably several resorts within easy driving distance. Most people book trips with the idea of skiing more than one mountain. It just adds variety."

"Like some of the golf trips I've taken, I suppose," Larry remarks.

Tammy nods. "Exactly. When you go to a golf resort with more than one course, you play as many different courses as you can, then you go back to the ones you like best. Skiing is the same. Most group travel packages spread out the skiing over several days as well as several mountains.

"This brings up an important point," Tammy continues. "Your transportation to and from the ski areas should be carefully planned. If you're renting a car or a van, make sure there's enough room for all the skiers and their equipment. Get a rental car with ski racks on the roof. Even if you're renting your equipment, chances are good you'll want to keep the same skis throughout the trip. That means transporting them to and from the slopes. Also, take into account the distance you'll have to walk from your car to the ski area. This could have a bearing on how much stuff you take with you. If parking is a twenty-minute hike from the lodge, you need to be aware of that before you take everything you own to the mountain."

"Don't they have valets or shuttles?" Larry inquires.

"The bigger mountains do, and every resort does its best to be accommodating. You just need to know the situation up front. Nothing is more annoying than showing up for your first day of fun and having a long unexpected hike just to get to the base."

Larry can picture himself lugging skis across a frozen tundra, dodging cars, skiers, and an occasional Saint Bernard along the way. He'll be sure to remember to check out the rental car and parking situations before boarding the plane.

"What other potential gremlins do I need to avoid?" he asks.

"Plenty of gremlins on the slopes, but nothing too major before you arrive," Tammy answers. "Are your lift tickets included as part of the travel package?"

"Lift what?"

"LIFT TICKETS. They're your passes to the slopes. In order to gain access to the ski areas, you purchase lift tickets. These allow you to use the mountains for a specified period of time. Tickets are usually sold for daily or multiple-day use, but even season passes can be purchased. Sometimes, one ticket is good for more than one mountain. The point is, there are a number of options when purchasing your lift tickets, so if your travel agent hasn't already done it for you, shop for the best deal."

"Are they really *tickets*?" Larry wants to know.

"Yes, they're tickets. They're either laminated or adhesive-backed. You wear them around your neck or mount them on your ski jacket. Just make sure they're clearly visible."

Larry writes this down. The last thing he needs is to lose his pass to this adventure.

"I'm sure I'm going to look like an accidental tourist," he declares.

"Nonsense," Tammy counters. "This is a vacation. Have a good time. Be a GAPER, and dare anybody to say anything."

"Be a *what?*"

"A gaper. That's what some of the locals call people who spend a lot of time looking around—gaping—when they get to the top of the mountain. Don't worry about it. Gape all you want. There's nothing more spectacular than turning off the lift toward your trail and seeing that spectacular vista and the whitest snow you've ever imagined, with a crisp wind filling your lungs as you stare out at the bluest sky. It's a wonderful experience. You'll know what I mean the first time you see it."

"A gaper, huh!" Larry pronounces.

They both laugh.

"One thing you need to be aware of, though, is the altitude."

"Why?" Larry asks.

"Your body is accustomed to living right here, at this altitude, which isn't very high relative to sea level. The elevations at ski resorts can range from one thousand to sixteen thousand feet above sea level. A severe change in altitude can be a shock to your system. An activity as simple as climbing a set of stairs at high altitude in ski boots can leave you huffing and puffing more than if you did the same amount of physical activity at sea level.

"Some people even experience ALTITUDE SICK-NESS. Its symptoms include headaches, nausea, dizziness, fatigue, and an increase in pulse rate. You might experience none of these symptoms, and there's no definitive elevation at which you start getting sick, but it's something you need to know."

"Yeah, I would hate to think I had food poisoning or something."

"Exactly," Tammy declares. "If you start getting these symptoms, be aware that it could be altitude sickness. Another possible cause is dehydration. Because of the cold temperatures and dry air, skiers often don't realize how quickly they burn the body's fuel and nutrients. It's especially important to drink water regularly throughout your ski day. This replenishes the body's reserves."

"Assuming I don't get sick, and before I gape at anything, I'm going to need some lessons," Larry mentions. "I don't even know how to stand and walk on skis. Cold wind and mountaintops are a long way away. I'm not even smart enough to know how to take a lesson."

"You're what ski instructors call a NEVER-EVER," she says. "You've never-ever skied before."

"I've never even considered it," Larry admits.

Tammy explains the basics of ski lessons to Larry, assuring him that virtually all resorts offer both group and individual lessons. She emphasizes that before Larry sets foot, ski, or pole on the slopes, he must take at least one lesson. Beginners who never get proper instruction usually develop bad habits that are very tough to break. Because on-site instruction is so convenient, she suggests he start out with a ski school group lesson. Then she tells Larry:

- Make sure you're in the right class. Ski schools offer a variety of classes based on skill level. Even beginner classes can be divided into two or three subdivisions and an absolute beginner needs to be sure he's in an absolute-beginner class. In most cases, these classes are identified by letters or numbers explained at the ski school reservation desk and at the gathering place for lessons. Many schools also show a continuously running video on television screens. This allows skiers to see different ability levels and rate their own abilities accordingly.

- Only take lessons from a certified ski instructor. Check the credentials of your instructor. Even though you probably have no idea what the accreditation means, the fact that an instructor has been certified by one of the sport's governing bodies is a good sign.

- Most ski classes consist of eight to twelve students depending on the time of year, the time of day, and how busy the ski area is. Try to get into a small group of learning skiers. You'll get more attention from the instructor, quickly develop friendships with other students, and probably improve faster.

"You mean as many as twelve other people are going to see how clumsy I am?" Larry asks.

"No, several hundred are," Tammy replies, laughing. "There will be a lot of people skiing around your class. Don't be embarrassed. I know that sounds impossible, but remember, you aren't alone. The other people in your beginner class will be just as nervous and self-conscious as you will be. Skiers are incredibly

INDIVIDUAL OR GROUP SKI SCHOOL

- GET IN THE RIGHT ONE
  FOR YOUR ABILITY.
- CHECK INSTRUCTOR'S
  CREDENTIALS.

patient and understanding of beginners. Most of them remember when they were in your boots."

"What if I complete the group lesson and I still don't get it?" Larry inquires. He's smiling, but his concern is obvious.

"I recommend that you take a series of group lessons," Tammy says, "because they guide your development. If you take only one lesson, the instructor won't be with you the next day when you can't remember a key piece of advice or when you're having trouble regaining the feel of a movement you thought you had learned.

"If you don't perform well in a group environment, consider taking private lessons. Be aware, though, that these one-on-one sessions are more expensive. Quite frankly, you might not get any more information out of a private beginner lesson than you do from a beginner ski school, but if you feel more comfortable dealing one-on-one with the instructor, by all means give it a shot. The important thing is, learn the basics correctly, get comfortable, ski within yourself, and have a good time."

"Good time," Larry repeats as he writes. His worried look hasn't completely evaporated, but he's a little more comfortable now that he knows what to expect.

"One final word of advice," Tammy pronounces as her phone rings. "Don't drink and ski. There's plenty of nightlife at the base. You might think a hot toddy will relax you and make you a better skier. That's wrong. Expect the opposite. Drinking lowers your body temperature, slows your reflexes, and can get you hurt. Don't do it."

"Yes, ma'am," Larry promises.

Tammy laughs, then says, "Excuse me a minute while I get this phone." She then steps behind the counter and picks up the receiver.

From a door behind the desk, a man in his late forties or early fifties steps out and extends his hand to Larry.

"Hi, I'm Jimmy Hugo. You must be Larry, our ski student."

"Does everyone know my plight today?" Larry wants to know.

"No," Jimmy says through a smile. "I work with Tammy and we discussed your visit before you arrived. Did you get everything you need?"

Larry holds up his trusty notepad. "I hope so. There is one question, however. Tammy said something about plenty of nightlife at the base. What kind of base was she talking about, and what kind of nightlife? What sort of clothes do I need to pack?"

Tammy is still on the phone, so Jimmy explains that BASE refers to the area at the bottom of the mountain, a hub of activity during day and night. Jimmy also informs him that he should pack casually. While there are a few exceptions, most ski areas are informal, and even the best restaurants are filled with patrons dressed in ski jackets and jeans. This nightlife activity is better known in skiing circles as APRÈS-SKI, referring to the social interaction that comes after a day on the slopes.

"The best advice I can give you is to check with the locals once you get to the ski resort," Jimmy says. "A few good questions can go a long way."

Tammy finishes her call in time to hear Jimmy's last words. "I wholeheartedly agree!" she echoes loudly. "I see you two have met."

"Yes," Larry responds. "Jimmy was just filling me in on the skier's nightlife. Hey, you mentioned one other thing I didn't quite understand. When you were calling me a gaper, you used the words *lift* and *trail*. I assume you mean the thing that gets me up the mountain and the trail on which I come back down. Is there anything special I should know about those?"

Tammy and Jimmy look at each other, then Jimmy motions Larry back toward the office door. "Come with me," he announces. "We aren't quite finished with you after all."

SEVEN

TRAILS AND TRIBULATIONS

Jimmy opens a filing cabinet and hands Larry three neatly folded brochures. When he unfolds them, Larry sees that they contain maps of different ski mountains with white trails branching downward like the legs of some giant arachnid.

"These are typical trail maps," Jimmy says. "Before you even consider getting on a lift, you need to pick up a trail map and study it. Otherwise, you have no idea where you're going, and that can be dangerous."

Larry studies one of the maps for a moment, then holds up his hands and shakes his head from side to side. "Where do I start? I have no idea how to read this."

Jimmy smiles. "Don't panic. The first thing you need to do is read the color key. TRAILS are marked by their level of difficulty. Usually, the never-ever beginner slope, or BUNNY SLOPE, is well marked and away from the larger trails. The bunny slope is a wide-open, gently sloping area where beginners learn technique and get a feel for the fundamentals. Finding it should be easy—it's usually close to the base. When you take your first lesson, that's where you'll be."

"And probably where I'll stay," Larry declares.

"Not necessarily," Jimmy tells him. "Most resorts have a good variety of beginner slopes. That's why it's important that you study the trail map. Beginner slopes are usually marked with GREEN CIRCLES on the trail map and on the directional signs along the trail itself. Before you go up, you need to plan your route down."

Larry writes feverishly. "You said green was beginner?" he asks.

"That's right," Jimmy affirms, before he explains the trail-marking colors:

- Green is the standard marking for easy beginner slopes.
- BLUE SQUARES indicate INTERMEDIATE RUNS, which usually are well-groomed, moderate slopes.
- A BLACK DIAMOND signifies advanced slopes.
- DOUBLE BLACK DIAMONDS denote expert slopes.

"In Europe," Jimmy adds, "they use the color red instead of the black-diamond classification, but that just emphasizes the point: *Check the map's key.*"

Larry nods.

"Also, don't assume that just because you start out on a BEGINNER TRAIL, you can forget the trail map and signs. Many trails intersect. If you aren't careful, you can make one wrong turn and end up on a black-diamond mogul run."

"Not the dreaded mogul," Larry says with a smile.

Jimmy smiles as well, but he turns serious again when he speaks. "Just remember, never take anything for granted. If you don't know exactly where you are, stop and read the map, or ask someone for directions. This sport is a lot of fun as long as you ski within your ability. Jump in over your head too quickly, and you're in for a miserable time."

"Duly noted," Larry declares.

"One last warning about trails and trail maps: Not only do you need to know where you're starting, you need to know where you're going to end up. Many resorts have trails that spur off to other areas of the mountain. Unless you plan carefully, you could end up on the opposite side of the mountain from where you want to be. You also could end up in a remote or isolated area. A snow-covered mountain at night is just as cold and lonely as it was four hundred years ago. Fortunately, ski patrollers make a 'sweep' of all trails, looking for stragglers, after the lifts close down for the day."

"Point made," Larry states as a chill runs over him.

Jimmy pauses for a moment before continuing by explaining some terms Larry will need to know relating to trails and trail conditions:

- GROOMED and UNGROOMED trails are just what the terms imply. Groomed trails have been groomed or smoothed out, and

TRAIL MAPS

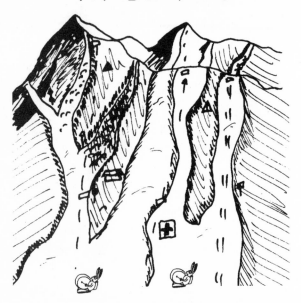

♦
♦ **DOUBLE BLACK DIAMOND SLOPE**
-VERY DIFFICULT-

♦ **BLACK DIAMOND SLOPE**
-DIFFICULT-

■ **INTERMEDIATE BLUE SLOPE**
-CHALLENGING-

● **BEGINNER GREEN SLOPE**
-EASY-

⊞ **FIRST AID**
-WHERE I WILL FINISH-

BUNNY SLOPE
-WHERE I WILL START-

-READ THE MAP BEFORE HITTING THE SLOPES-

-BE CAREFUL AT INTERSECTIONS-

-KNOW WHERE YOU WANT TO END UP-

ungroomed trails have been left untouched after a storm or a previous ski day. As you learn the fundamentals of skiing, you need to stay on groomed trails.

- POWDER is another term you'll hear or read about. It describes newly fallen, dry snow. Skiing in fresh powder is great fun, but it requires technique modifications best done after you've reached the intermediate ability level. Now that's not to say that you shouldn't ski on freshly fallen snow. Exactly the opposite is true. Nothing is better than a day on fresh snow. Just remember to stick to the groomed trails for a while. And look for the term PACKED POWDER, which refers to powder that has been groomed.

- The antithesis of fresh powder is CRUD. As the word implies, it's generally an unpleasant, slushy mixture of melting snow and ice that forms on warm days, usually in the spring. Skiing on crud requires more effort than skiing groomed snow, and you'll find a great deal of inconsistency in your skiing. Skis sometimes hang in the crud or get mired in the slush, and this can cause serious accidents. Be careful.

- You might also ski a mountain that has man-made snow. That's artificial snow made by pumping water up the mountain through pipes, then spraying it under intense pressure through large fans into the cold air. The fine water droplets freeze and become snow CRYSTALS before hitting the ground. Man-made snow is

heavier and has a different consistency than natural snow, but it allows many ski areas to open
earlier in the season as well as to operate at
near-full capacity during stretches of cold days
when snow isn't falling. You just need to know
what you're skiing. If it's man-made snow, expect it to be a little icier and a little harder.

- There's another use for the aforementioned
  word *base.* In ski reports, the term BASE doesn't
  refer to the bottom of the mountain. It describes the depth of the snow coverage on
  most slopes. For example, a thirty-inch base
  simply means that thirty inches of snow cover
  most of the trails. Depending on where you
  go, you might be shocked by how much snow
  accumulates on the mountains.

As Larry reviews his notes, he sees one important thing still missing. "We've talked about all the
elements I'm likely to encounter going *down* the
mountain," he says, "but the one thing I don't know
is how I get *up* the mountain."

"LIFTS," Jimmy answers.

"Okay, what are lifts, and how do I use them?"

Jimmy proceeds to explain that lifts are the machines that transport skiers up the mountain:

- The most common is the CHAIRLIFT. It's just
  that—a chair attached to a moving cable suspended above the ground. It carries you on an
  ascent to your desired trail. Most of the lifts
  you see at today's resorts are chairlifts. Each
  chair carries from two to four skiers.

KNOW YOUR SNOW

GROOMED-SMOOTH
POWDER-NEWLY FALLEN, LIGHT SNOW
CRUD-SLUSHY SNOW AND ICE
PACKED POWDER-LIGHT SNOW THAT HAS BEEN GROOMED
MAN-MADE SNOW-TECHNOLOGY IMITATING NATURE!

- There are also TOW-LIFTS, although they don't lift you off the ground. Instead, they tow, or pull, you up the slope. Some beginner slopes have tow-lifts, so pay close attention in ski school to the lift LOADING and UNLOADING procedures. The main type of tow-lift is called a POMA. It consists of a metal bar with a disk at its end suspended from a moving cable. To LOAD, you place this disk between your legs and let it rest against your buttocks. Don't sit back; let the lift pull you up the slope. Other TOW-LIFTS include ROPE TOWS and T-BARS, but most resorts have phased these older types of lifts out of service.

- Then there are GONDOLAS, or enclosed cabins. These vary in size and speed. They can transport anywhere from two to ten skiers uphill and are generally much faster and more comfortable than chairlifts. Gondolas can be very nice—some are even heated—but they are usually reserved for longer lifts.

- Finally, many large resorts feature TRAMS, the granddaddies of all lifts. Some hold well over one hundred skiers in an enclosed cabin that's quickly transported to the top of the mountain via moving cable.

"No gondolas or trams on the bunny slopes?" Larry asks.

Jimmy laughs. "Sorry, but no." Jimmy then explains a few of the points about lifts to remember when loading and unloading. He instructs Larry to:

TYPES OF SKI LIFTS

ROPE

POMA

CHAIRLIFT

-PAY ATTENTION
WHEN LOADING
AND UNLOADING.

-WATCH OTHERS TO
SEE HOW IT IS DONE.

GONDOLA

TRAM

- Observe proper etiquette when approaching a LIFT LINE (the queue you get in to load onto the lift). Don't ski fast near the lift line and don't cut in front of someone else in line. Lift lines are usually roped off, so always be aware of where you are relative to the lift line. Don't get too close to the person in front of you, and don't cross skis with anyone else. That damages skis and causes accidents.

- Be ready when it's your turn to load. Move up to the loading area and be ready to get onto the chair, enter the gondola, or take hold of the poma bar. Most lifts don't stop for loading and unloading. It's your job to be ready.

- Always keep one hand free when loading onto any lift. Hold your poles securely in one hand, and use your free hand to properly position yourself onto the lift. When unloading, get out of the way quickly. People will be unloading behind you, and the top of the lift is no place for loitering. Move out of the way of unloading traffic and ready yourself for your run.

"Oh, and don't stick your tongue to anything metal on the lift. It will freeze and stick," Jimmy warns.

"What?"

Jimmy laughs heartily. "Just kidding. The main point is don't be intimidated by lifts, but don't be stupid about them either. Pay attention to your ski instructor, watch how others get on and off, and be ready when it's your turn. Lifts aren't amusement park rides. They don't stop just because you dropped a glove, so be careful."

Larry finishes writing this down and realizes the lesson is over. He stands and thanks Jimmy for all his help.

The two men walk back to the outer lobby where Tammy is waiting with another note for Larry.

"This is a good friend of mine who owns a fitness center here in town," she explains, pointing to the name and address written on the note. "I've called him. He knows you're coming."

"I am?" Larry inquires.

"If you have time. You really need to see him. He's an expert on ski conditioning and winter sport exercises. You'll enjoy yourself a lot more if you're in good shape before you go. There are plenty of simple exercises you should try before hitting the slopes."

Larry looks at his watch and decides the afternoon is shot anyway, so he might as well learn all he can. He thanks Tammy and Jimmy and moves on to his next destination.

SKI LIFT ETIQUETTE:

- DON'T BREAK IN LINE.

- BE AWARE OF OTHERS' SKIS
  (DON'T CROSS SOMEONE'S SKIS).

- BE READY WHEN IT'S TIME TO LOAD.

- KEEP ONE HAND FREE WHEN LOADING
  ONTO A LIFT.

- GET ON AND OFF AS QUICKLY AND
  SAFELY AS POSSIBLE.

EIGHT

SKI CONDITIONING

The health club is less than a mile away. Larry quickly drives there, parks his car in the half-full lot, and follows two young, exceptionally healthy women through the front door and into the lobby, where another smiling woman in tights greets him and directs him to the aerobics room. The instructor he's to meet is finishing a class. Larry waits inside the large, mirrored room while the class files out.

A stocky man in a stretch bodysuit catches Larry's glance and approaches with an outstretched, sweaty hand.

"Are you Larry?" the man asks.

"Yes. Are you William?"

"Bill," the stocky man answers. "Bill Kiddly. William is way too formal."

Larry smiles. When he takes a closer look, he sees that even though this man is well into his forties, he still has the body of a teenage athlete. His arms and legs show the well-defined lines of regimented workouts. His face is weathered and his hairline shows his age, but his eyes dance with energy. *This lesson is going to be fun*, Larry decides.

"Bill, I appreciate your seeing me on such short notice—"

"No problem," Bill interrupts, waving away Larry's concern with both hands. "I understand you're going skiing."

"In one month," Larry admits, "and I started the day knowing absolutely nothing about the sport."

"So, I take it that you know *more* than nothing now?"

Larry holds up his notepad. "I take good notes."

"Well," Bill continues, "has anyone talked to you about exercise?"

Larry shakes his head. "That's why I'm here."

"Great," Bill says as he wipes his forehead with a towel. "First, let's talk about your current workout routine. Do you have a standard exercise program?"

"Not really. I swim, play tennis and golf, and occasionally get in a pickup basketball game."

"That's all good, but you need to increase and streamline your exercise habits for the next thirty days if you want to ski effectively."

"Hold on just a second here," Larry demurs. "I don't want to hurt or embarrass myself, and I hope I'll have a good time. I don't expect to be very effective."

"Sure you do!" Bill exclaims with gusto. "Effectiveness is a relative term. For your skill level, you want to be as effective and efficient as possible. That requires a certain amount of conditioning. Of course, you're not training to be a championship racer, but you should do a few simple things to make your trip more enjoyable."

Larry gets the notepad ready. "Enjoyable is what I'm after," he concedes.

"Okay," Bill goes on. "Always keep in mind that skiing is a dynamic sport. You are constantly reacting to your environment, your equipment, and your own body, so the better conditioned you are, the more effective you will be. You said you swim?"

"That's right," Larry answers.

"Well, you should swim laps regularly between now and your trip. This will help with your conditioning. Skiing is much like swimming in that you have to respond to your environment. If you fight the water, you tire easily and get nowhere. The same is true with skiing. If you fight the slopes, you tire quickly and have little or no chance of having a good time. If, on the other hand, you prepare yourself and hone your reflexes, you have a greater opportunity to enjoy yourself."

"So, I should swim. How about running?"

"Running is good, but it's not the most time-effective exercise you could choose. Running is great for your cardiovascular system, but so are aerobics and cycling, and those activities help out in other ski-related areas, such as flexibility and lower-body stamina."

"Swim, bike, and do aerobics," Larry murmurs as he writes. "No running."

Bill also reminds Larry that effective skiing requires all elements of conditioning:

- strength,
- stamina,
- and flexibility.

"And no one is more important than the other," Bill declares. "You can have a weight lifter's strength, but if you tire easily and have no flexibility, you won't be very effective. The same is true of all the conditioning elements. You can have ironman stamina, but it's only as good as your strength and suppleness on the slopes. And if you have both strength and flexibility but no stamina, you'll have a few good runs, then be too tired to finish the day."

"How do I get in shape for skiing in just one month?" Larry wants to know. "I'm not sure I have any of those elements."

"Oh, sure you do," Bill assures him. "If you exercise regularly, you're already in decent enough condition to enjoy skiing at some level. Of course, improving your workout regimen will get you closer to realizing your full potential as a skier."

Larry smiles at the reference to his full potential as a skier. "Okay, what do I need to do?"

Bill explains that in order to get the most benefit from his workout, Larry must incorporate as many dynamic elements into the exercises as possible, while simulating some of the motions and activities that he'll experience on the slopes.

"Do you own a pair of in-line skates?" Bill asks.

"No."

"You should consider buying a pair. The balancing aspects of in-line skating, along with its turning techniques and lower-body workout, all combine for great ski conditioning. Also consider:

- SKI SIMULATORS. These can be as simple as a balancing board or as complex as an edging simulator. Also, try a cross-country simulator, if you can. Not only will it give you an idea of what to expect if you decide to cross-country ski for a day, but Nordic machines give you a great workout even if you're Alpine skiing.

- Also look into WATER AEROBICS. In terms of strength, endurance, and adapting to your environment, there are few better fitness regimens.

- Finally, consider YOGA. Thirty days is a short window to accomplish much, but yoga builds strength and flexibility while also focusing your powers of concentration—all of which are critical elements in skiing.

"Wow, this is quite an agenda," Larry declares. "You know, I do work for a living. I can't just drop everything and go on a thirty-day workout sabbatical."

"You don't have to," Bill quickly points out. "Remember, you're not trying to be an expert the first time out. Thirty minutes a day combining some elements of strength conditioning, stamina, and stretching will be plenty. If you commit half-an-hour a day to your workout, you'll have a much better time when you get to the slopes."

"Fair enough," Larry admits. "Are there any exercises I can do?"

GET IN SHAPE!

WORK ON STRENGTH, STAMINA, AND FLEXIBILITY TOGETHER.

- BIKING
- SWIMMING
- IN-LINE SKATING
- SKI SIMULATORS
- AEROBICS
- YOGA

LARRY
AFTER
TRAINING

LARRY BEFORE TRAINING

Bill explains that there are many ski-specific exercises used to train and condition skiers of all abilities. They include:

- Balancing on a board. Stand on your toes on top of a two-by-four, and in slow, deliberate motions, bend your knees to a full crouch position, then stand up and reach as high as you can. Repeating this process several times increases your balance and strengthens your legs.
- Boot simulation. Wearing your ski boots, sidestep up and down a staircase. This exercise not only prepares you for what it feels like to wear ski boots, it also prepares your legs for some of the motions you will experience on the slopes.
- Wall twist. Place both hands against a wall in front of you, and hop from one foot to the other, while twisting your hips from side to side. This simulates turning and prepares your body for what should become a natural reflex on the slopes.

"There are hundreds of other exercises," Bill continues. "Entire books have been devoted to ski conditioning, and even the experts debate the best methods. One thing's not disputed, however: *The better conditioned you are, the better skier you'll become.*"

Larry writes down that last statement and puts it in quotes. If nothing else, he has a good axiom to take with him on his thirty-day quest to better fitness.

"Has anyone spoken to you about lessons?" Bill asks.

Larry lowers his notepad to his side and says, "Tammy gave me an overview of how to enroll in ski school and how to take a lesson, but as far as getting any picture of the type of instruction I'm likely to get, I'm clueless."

Bill rubs his chin for a moment and ponders Larry's situation before continuing. "Well, there's only so much instruction you can handle before actually getting onto the snow, but in order to fully appreciate the exercises I've told you about, you need to know what you're trying to accomplish and why."

"That *would* be helpful," Larry acknowledges.

"The first thing you need to do is familiarize yourself with your ski equipment—"

Larry quickly raises his hand to interrupt. "Wait a minute. I spent the better part of the day with the staff at Ski Masters." Larry proudly holds up his notepad filled with the information he diligently wrote down. "I'm not an equipment expert, but I know enough to get properly outfitted."

Bill nods. "Good, but you still need to spend some time using your equipment on the snow before you take your first lesson. Remember, skiing is a dynamic sport, full of action working with and against the forces of nature.

"That notepad of yours is certainly going to be helpful, but it won't tell you how you're going to feel out on the snow. For that, you need to put on your boots and skis and spend some time getting accustomed to the sensation of moving around on the slippery stuff. You should plan to arrive at the mountain well before your lesson is scheduled and get used to the equipment and the weather conditions.

"In fact," Bill continues, "if you buy or rent skis and boots, and you get the opportunity, I'd suggest that you actually wear them at home or in your hotel room for short periods of time. First, while wearing your ski boots, walk up a flight of stairs sideways as I described a few minutes ago. Lift one boot up a stair, then lift the next alongside, and continue until you reach the top. Turn to face the opposite direction and sidestep back down the stairs."

"That sure sounds like a good workout," Larry says.

"It is," Bill replies. "Next, snap yourself into your skis and walk around on a carpet to get a feel for their length, weight, and maneuverability. You'll quickly discover that small steps are the most efficient and that changing direction involves, first, moving one ski out at an angle to the other and then moving the other alongside."

Larry chuckles at the image of himself stumbling around his living room while wearing ski gear. "Boy, I'll have to make sure I pull the curtains so my neighbors won't be able to see me," he says.

"Believe me, the effort will pay off," Bill says.

Larry writes a reminder to try the stair climb and carpet ski shuffle. "What else should I know before getting out on the hill?" he asks.

"Well, one of the reasons for the specific exercises I've recommended is that when you ski, you constantly deal with natural forces such as gravity and friction. Gravity, of course, tries to pull you down the hill and, believe it or not, there's friction between your skis' bases and the snow."

"You mean, the skis rub against the snow enough to slow them down?" Larry asks, surprised.

"That's right," Bill says. "The amount of friction isn't great, but it's enough to actually melt a thin film of snow as the ski rubs across the snow surface. In fact, if your ski bases aren't waxed well, the friction can really build up and slow you down."

"That sounds exactly like what I need," Larry says. "Maybe I should sandpaper my skis!"

"Oh no," Bill quickly cautions. "If your skis don't slide smoothly, you'll never be able to learn how to make a controlled turn. A ski with a rough base will be unstable, and you'll really have to fight to keep your balance."

"Okay, how will I be able to keep gravity from pulling me down the hill like a runaway train?"

Bill smiles at Larry's question, for it's the most common one asked by timid new skiers. "While your instructor will go into more detail in your lesson, you need to understand the fall line and what it means to set an edge."

Bill walks over to one side of the room and picks up a racquetball. Moving to a large exercise mat, he lifts one corner and says, "Imagine that this mat is a ski slope."

Larry nods and looks on with interest.

"The fall line is the shortest, straightest, and steepest line down any slope," Bill says. "It's the path of least resistance."

Bill holds the ball on the corner of the mat he has lifted, then he lets it roll freely down to the opposite side. "The ball has just followed the fall line of the mat's slope," he says.

"So, the fall line is just what the name implies—it's the way gravity would take an object if it fell," Larry says.

"Exactly," Bill replies before he walks over to retrieve the ball. Next, he picks up a small trash can and places it on the mat, near the mat's edge. Bill then says, "The reason it's important to understand the fall line is because you don't want to be taking a direct line down the slope. If you do, you will just keep gaining speed."

Bill again holds up the corner of the mat and releases the ball, just like before. This time, though, the ball rolls and bounces hard off the trash can. At that, Bill adds, "It's very important that you control your speed and direction."

Larry can picture himself as the ball, only, in his case, he would be ramming into a forest of trees instead of a trash can. "I get the point," he says with a sheepish grin.

"Good," Bill says. "That's one of the reasons why I've emphasized lower-body exercises such as the stair climb. That one in particular conditions your legs for turning and setting an edge against the fall line."

Larry jots down a few more notes before glancing up to ask, "What do you mean by 'setting an edge'?"

Bill smiles and figures the best way to describe this to Larry is with another demonstration. He asks

Larry to stand on the mat near its corner. Bill lifts the other end of the mat, forcing Larry to dig the "uphill" edges of his shoes into the soft mat to keep from tumbling over.

"Can you feel yourself automatically distributing your weight and edging your shoes?" Bill asks.

"Yes," Larry responds.

"Good," Bill says. "Had you been wearing skis, and had the mat been an actual ski slope, you'd be setting an edge into the snow, creating a small but solid platform on which you'd be able to stand motionless. It's one of the first things you'll learn in ski school. Its resultant stability reassures first-time skiers. It's also something you can condition yourself to do long before you ever arrive at the mountain."

Larry steps off the mat and says, "Okay, let's say I get a good feel for setting an edge. I'm still going to fall, right?"

"Sure you will," Bill replies.

"So how do I keep from hurting myself?" Larry asks, motioning toward the trash can to make his point. "I mean, I'm going to fall the way gravity pulls me. No amount of exercise can stop that."

"You're right," Bill says. "But knowing how to fall can help."

Larry, perplexed, looks up from his notes and asks, "But wouldn't my falling, by its own definition, mean that I am out of control?"

Bill nods. "True, but even if you're off balance and out of control, you still can minimize the severity of your fall by falling on your side, if possible."

SETTING AN EDGE

·IMAGINE SOMEONE IS TRYING TO
PULL YOU DOWNHILL.
·TO KEEP FROM BEING PULLED OVER, DIG YOUR
SKIS' UPHILL EDGES INTO THE SNOW.

"I'd think the fastest way to stop would be to sit down on my big rear end and skid quickly to a stop," Larry says, grinning while patting his derriere.

"Actually, sitting down backward is probably the worst thing you can do if you're out of control," Bill says. "By pressuring the tails of your skis, you'll pick up even more speed and lose any ability to steer with the fronts of your skis. You can also severely strain your knees and suffer a serious injury. So if you lose control, fall onto your side."

Larry writes down the advice in capital letters. "Now I know how to set an edge and how to fall. How will I be able to move down the fall line under control?"

"Your instructor will probably teach you how to make basic snowplow turns to start," Bill says.

Larry looks up, recalling that Phil had mentioned something earlier at his store about a snowplow. "What is that?" Larry asks. "I assume we're not talking about road equipment here."

Bill chuckles. "No, you won't be plowing the streets, but, in a sense, you will be plowing the snow as you slide downhill. The snowplow is a high-friction turning technique that gives beginning skiers exceptional control over speed and direction."

"Now you've *really* got my attention," Larry says.

"In a snowplow stance the feet and skis are spaced apart a little more than shoulder width," Bill explains, demonstrating what he means by standing with his legs apart, his feet pointed inward. "The ski tips are angled toward each other, forming a wedgelike shape. By pressuring the inside edges of both skis equally—which, in effect, plows the snow off to the sides—you can ski straight down even a moderate slope at a slow, controlled speed. Apply even more edge pressure and you'll stop.

"And here's the cool part that gives new skiers a real sense of accomplishment: If you pressure one ski edge more than the other, you'll start to turn slowly toward the other side. In other words, if you press down on the inside edge of your right ski more than the left, you'll turn to the left. Pressure the left ski and you'll turn right."

"Now I understand why you put so much emphasis on building lower-body strength," Larry says. "You really have to use your legs a lot. Any other conditioning tips?"

"Have no fear, take a deep breath, and ski well," Bill suggests.

"Thanks, I'll try."

Bill wipes his forehead again and looks at the wall for a moment. "There is one thing I need to ask you."

"Sure," Larry replies.

"You said earlier you didn't want to hurt or embarrass yourself. You're going to fall, but, unless you act foolishly, that will only hurt your pride. Has anyone explained the SKI CODE?"

"No, is that anything like Morse Code?" Larry asks.

SNOWPLOW

SNOWPLOW IS A SLOW TECHNIQUE FOR BEGINNERS.

Bill laughs. "It's not that kind of code. The Ski Code is a code of conduct, sort of like ski etiquette. If you don't want to embarrass yourself, you need to know how to act."

"By all means," Larry declares. "Give me the code."

NINE

FALLING POLITELY

Knowing that it will take a while to explain the Ski Code, Bill motions for Larry to accompany him to a couple of chairs in the corner where they can continue the discussion.

"At ski areas hundreds of people of vastly different skill levels come down the mountain at the same time," Bill begins. "Without some uniform code of acceptable conduct, this can present problems."

"Sort of like driving with no traffic laws," Larry suggests.

Bill nods. "Imagine driving in hazardous conditions with no marked lanes and no speed limits, sharing a road with everything from family station wagons to Indy cars. That's what skiing would be like without the Ski Code or some other recognized rules of behavior."

Larry resumes his note-taking. "How do I keep from violating the code?"

"First, you need to recognize that skiing etiquette is largely a function of common sense. If you
are out of control on a crowded slope, somebody is
likely to get hurt. Like everything else in skiing, the
rules of safety and etiquette are dynamic—they depend largely on the snow conditions, the level of activity on the slopes, your skill level, and the skill
levels of others around you. To ski safely and politely, you have to be aware of all these variables."

Bill then proceeds to explain that, in order to ski
safely, there are some simple rules that must be followed:

- Always check your ski equipment before
  going out on the slopes. Make sure your bindings are properly and professionally adjusted.
  Check your skis for any damage or abrasions,
  particularly on their BASES, or bottoms. Spend
  time in your boots and adjust their fit features
  to ensure they work the way they should. Finally, go through a preskiing checklist of your
  apparel and accessories to make sure you've
  got everything in order before arriving at the
  mountain.

- Always warm up and stretch your muscles before going out on the slopes. Like any athletic
  endeavor, the risk of injury goes down when
  you've properly prepared yourself. A ten- to
  fifteen-minute workout, with an emphasis on
  stretching, will make your ski experience safer
  and more pleasant.

- Ski within the limits of your ability. In other

words, stay in control. Falling is a natural part of skiing. In order to improve, a skier has to push the limits of his or her ability to a point, but that point should never go beyond what is safe.

- Stop skiing when you're tired. Most accidents occur when you've stayed on the slopes one run too long. This is why a pretrip exercise routine is important to better skiing. By improving your conditioning, you lengthen the amount of time you can spend on the mountain.

- Be cautious in bad weather. Conditions on a snow-covered mountain can change quickly and dramatically. Don't be caught off guard. If visibility decreases or you experience a WHITE-OUT during a snowstorm—when visibility is almost zero—slow down and ski over to the side of the trail. Stop and wait for visibility to improve, or ski slowly along the trees at the edge of the trail, using them for visual reference.

- Choose a safe route. Read all signs and markings, steer clear of hazardous areas or closed runs, and watch yourself in icy areas or locations where AVALANCHES might occur.

Larry looks up from his notes. "Did you say 'avalanches'?"

"Yes," Bill says. His face is firm and fixed, and his tone serious. Clearly, this is a no-nonsense subject. "Almost all fatal ski accidents are from avalanches. In fact, Bud Werner, a U.S. Ski Team member in the early 1960s, was killed in an avalanche, so even the experts should beware. As a beginner, if you stay on well-groomed trails, the likelihood of being in an avalanche is very small, but don't rule it out. It's difficult to predict where or when avalanches will occur."

"What do I do to avoid them?" Larry asks.

"Check the SKI PATROL's report before you go out—"

"Whoa. The ski what?"

"Ski Patrol," Bill repeats. "Members of this group are, in effect, a ski area's police, rescue squad, and safety inspectors rolled into one. They go out before the slopes open and check conditions. They close slopes that are dangerous. They ski the entire area from top to bottom after lifts close to make sure the trails are clear of skiers. They'll even intentionally trigger avalanches before anyone gets out on the mountain."

"That makes sense," Larry says.

Bill nods. "Yes, it does. One of the first things you should do when you get to a mountain is identify the Ski Patrol. They usually wear red parkas with a large cross on them. The Ski Patrol gets you off the mountain if you have a serious accident, so they're good people to know."

"That's another point I hadn't even considered," Larry mentions. "I guess if you get hurt out there, you can't pull an ambulance onto the slope and hop in."

"You're right. Sometimes the logistics of getting an injured skier off the mountain are more trying than the injuries themselves."

"Now, what about this Ski Code?" Larry asks. "I want to do the right thing out there. What do I need to know?"

Bill pauses, realizing that these are important points. He wants to make sure he gives Larry good information in terms he can understand.

"The Ski Code is the internationally recognized guide for skier conduct," Bill explains. "The rules are simple, and, for the most part, reflect common sense, but they are all very important."

"Sometimes common sense is not very common," Larry interjects.

"You've got that right," Bill declares. "Never assume people around you understand the rules. It's just like driving your car—be aware of the people around you, because you can never anticipate what someone else is going to do."

Bill then proceeds to explain to Larry the basic rules outlined in the Ski Code:

- Always ski in a manner that does not endanger others. Never put anyone else at risk. This is the Golden Rule of skiing: Ski around others the way you would have them ski around you.

- Ski within yourself. Adapt your skiing to your ability as well as the prevailing weather and terrain.

- If you are approaching another skier from behind, choose a route that does not endanger that skier. Remember, skiers are focusing on the terrain ahead of them. They don't have the time or ability to focus on someone coming up from behind. The same is true for snowboarders. Remember that they have a different blind spot than do skiers. Choose your course wisely.

- When passing or overtaking another skier, give the skier in front of you a wide berth. If you're too close, he or she could turn into you, causing a serious accident. The person in front always has the right of way.

- Don't cross or enter a trail, or restart after stopping, without first making sure no skiers are nearby. This is sort of like being careful not to run across the interstate without first checking for cars. But you would be amazed how many skiers jump out into merging trails without looking.

- You should never stop in dangerous places, even though narrow passages or low-visibility places are where you want to stop and admire the scenery. You also shouldn't stop in the middle of a trail. Move to the side when you want to take a break, and if you fall, get out of the way quickly.

- If you are climbing uphill, use the side of the trail. If your glove or glasses fall off while you're skiing, the temptation is to climb up quickly, pick up the items, and be on your way. That's like going the wrong way down the middle of a one-way street. Unless skiers uphill have a clear view of what you're doing, don't try it. Get to the side of the trail and walk up.

- Observe all the trail signs and Ski Patrol warnings. Don't ski a closed trail or ski fast in a slow-ski zone. Just do what you're told and everybody will have a good time.

- If you see an accident, stop and determine if you can help. Get word to the Ski Patrol of any serious injuries. If you don't ski well enough to look for help on your own, flag down a better skier and ask him or her to locate emergency personnel. This is another Golden Rule of skiing: Look out for others as you would have them look out for you.

Larry writes these down, and it dawns on him after a few moments that Bill has stopped talking. "Is that it?" Larry asks.

"That's it. That's the Ski Code," Bill says.

Larry reads through his notes. "You're right, it *is* common sense."

"Uncommonly practiced sometimes, however," Bill adds.

Larry looks back at all the notes he's taken throughout the day. "Bill, this has been great. Can you think of anything else I need to know before making this trek?"

Bill looks thoughtfully at the ceiling, wipes his forehead again, then motions Larry to follow him. "Come on. I have something in my office that might help."

When they arrive, Larry notices more photos of plummeting skiers in brightly colored suits. This time he doesn't ask which one is Bill. He's not sure he wants to know.

Bill reaches into a desk drawer and takes out a small, worn book with frayed edges. "This is a glossary of ski terms I've pulled together over the years.

WHEN FALLING DOWN, DO IT POLITELY.

-KNOW THE SKI CODE-

-GIVE THOSE IN FRONT A WIDE BERTH.

-DO NOT WALK UP THE MIDDLE OF THE SLOPE.

-HELP OTHERS.

-CHECK BEFORE MERGING.

-USE COMMON SENSE!

-FOLLOW THE CODE!

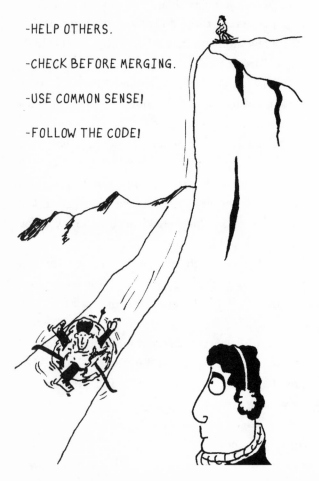

Back when I taught lessons, I used to give this out to beginning skiers. You might get something like it at your first ski school. If not, you'll have a head start on the rest of your class."

Larry thumbs through the glossary as he and Bill walk back to the front of the health club. He's already heard many of the glossary's words and phrases—through the courtesy of Bill, Jimmy, Tammy, Tommy, Pic, and Phil—and he has to stop himself from reading when they get to the front door.

"Bill, this is great," Larry says. "You've been a huge help. I can't thank you enough."

"Sure you can," Bill responds. "Go out there, have fun, and ski well. That's all the thanks any teacher needs."

Larry shakes Bill's extended hand. "I'll do my best," he promises, as he walks out the door and heads back to his car.

On the way back to his office, he thinks of Jennifer and all the things he needs to accomplish in the next thirty days. "I'll do my best," he reaffirms, to no one in particular.

Ten

A Groomed Ending

Larry and Jennifer sit in front of a huge roaring fire inside the atrium of the ski lodge. It's their last day on the slopes, and the trip has been a grand success.

Everyone, including Jennifer, is surprised by how well Larry has progressed. By the end of the third day, he routinely skied the intermediate slopes, and he took his first snowboarding lesson. He made a number of new friends, all of whom extended open invitations for him to come back any time. He was scared, as expected, and he had more than one yard sale, as expected. He only experienced altitude sickness for a few hours on the first day, and the symptoms were relatively mild. But he *did* gape for several minutes on his first few runs, finding the beauty of the mountains breathtaking and spectacular. Larry's only disappointment is that he waited so long to experience the rush of skiing and all that goes with it.

Jennifer couldn't be happier. Her office friends found Larry to be the life of the trip, and even her boss, an avid skier, commented on how nice it was to have a beginner along who had really done his homework.

She pats Larry's knee and sips her hot coffee as they gaze out the large window at skiers coming down a web of white trails. "This has been wonderful," she announces. "I don't know what could make this trip any better."

Larry reaches into the pocket of his ski jacket and pulls out a ring box. "How 'bout this?" he asks as he hands it to her.

"Oh, Larry!" she exclaims as she opens it.

"How would you feel about marrying a ski bum?"

"Larry, this is wonderful. Of course...I mean, yes. I would love to marry a ski bum, as long as it's you."

They kiss, and dozens of skiers near them erupt into cheers and applause. The waitress brings a huge cake with "Best Wishes" written in white icing and two small plastic skiers carving their way toward the edge.

At first Jennifer is speechless, then she finally demands, "How long have you been planning this?"

"Since the day you talked me into taking this trip."

"So, where do you want to go on our honeymoon?"

"Wherever there's snow and some radical runs," Larry declares.

Jennifer kisses him again, realizing that winters are going to be a lot different from now on.

ELEVEN

BILL'S GLOSSARY

advanced ski. Longer and stiffer than a recreational ski, used by expert skiers.

advanced skier. An expert skier.

aerials. A type of freestyle or acrobatic skiing where skiers perform acrobatic twists, flips, and turns while in the air. A very dramatic and very dangerous form of competitive skiing.

afterbody. The rear of a ski. (*see also* **tail**)

Alpine skiing. Downhill skiing, as opposed to Nordic, or cross-country, skiing. Downhill skiers are propelled by gravity, Nordic skiers by physical effort on flat terrain.

altitude sickness. The body's adverse reaction to a dramatic change in elevation. Symptoms include headaches, shortness of breath, dizziness, nausea, and rapid heart rate.

après-ski. The social activity—*i.e.,* the nightlife—following a day on the slopes.

artificial snow. Man-made, or mechanically made snow, created by pumping a fine spray of water at high pressure into cold air. Artificial snow is denser and packs harder than natural snow.

avalanche. A mass of snow sliding rapidly downhill that creates an often deadly situation for anyone in its path.

ballet. A form of freestyle skiing in which the skier actually dances, much like a figure skater.

base. (1) The bottom of the mountain where the ski lodge is situated. (2) The average depth of snow coverage on a mountain. (3) The smooth, waxed running surface on the bottom of a ski.

basket. The plastic disk near the end of the ski pole that keeps the tip from penetrating too far into the snow.

beginner. Someone who is learning to ski.

beginner ski. A short, flexible ski designed to be forgiving of mistakes.

beginner trails. The easier trails on a mountain. Recommended for beginning skiers, usually marked by green circles.

biathlon. A Nordic ski competition that combines the elements of cross-country skiing and firearms marksmanship.

binding. The mechanism that attaches the boot to the ski, which releases under the pressures created in awkward or hard falls. The most complex piece of ski equipment.

black diamond. An advanced slope, marked on trail maps and signage by a single black diamond.

blue square. The designation for an intermediate slope, marked on ski resort trail maps and signage.

bunny slope. The most gently sloping run on the mountain, usually close to the base lodge. Primarily for first-time skiers.

camber. The arch or bow built into a ski that absorbs the weight of the skier and distributes it equally along the ski's length.

carving. Efficient turning on the inside edge of the downhill ski.

catching an edge. An accident where the edge of a ski digs and catches in the snow, causing a fall. Frequently caused by an unseen rut or chunks of frozen snow.

center of gravity. A skier's dynamic balance point, usually located in the body's midsection for men, lower in the hips for women.

chairlift. The most common type of ski lift. Chairs are fixed to a moving cable that is suspended above the ground.

code, or Ski Code. The international rules of behavior when skiing.

combined. A separate Alpine racing competition in which slalom times and downhill times for individual racers are added together and then ranked. Most of the world's best ski racers specialize in one or two events (slalom, giant slalom, super-G, or downhill), and skiers that do well in combined competition are considered especially well rounded.

competition. A race or other event on skis.

competition ski. The longest and stiffest of the four major types of skis. Used by experts for racing.

cornice. An overhanging ridge of snow.

cross-country, or Nordic, skiing. The earliest type of skiing, dating back some forty-five hundred years, in which skiers propel themselves over flat and rolling terrain.

crud. Heavy, slushy snow conditions caused by warm-weather melting.

crust. A hard surface of snow covering a softer underlayer. Caused by thawing and refreezing cycles.

crystals. Snowflakes that thaw and refreeze, forming a sparkling sheen on the surface of the snow.

descent. The route downhill.

double black diamond. The most difficult expert slopes, marked on maps and signage by two black diamonds.

double pole push. Planting both poles in the snow and pushing off to propel oneself forward.

downhill racing. An event in which racers attempt to record the fastest time during a single run on a course with a minimum number of gates. Speeds often exceed seventy miles per hour.

drag lift or **tow-lift.** A surface transport that pulls or tows skiers uphill.

dual-lens goggles. Goggles with two pairs of lenses separated by a layer of air and ventilated to reduce fogging during a ski run.

edges. The metal strips on either side of a ski that protect its base and bite into the snow during a turn.

edging. Tilting the skis on edge to turn.

expert. The most advanced category of skier.

expert runs. The most difficult trails at a ski area. Usually marked by double black diamonds.

fall line. The shortest, straightest, and steepest line down any slope. The path of least resistance a ball would follow if rolled down the slope.

fanny pack. A small bag worn around the waist.

F.I.S. The Federation Internationale de Ski, the international governing body of skiing.

flex. The degree to which a ski bends from tip to tail when pressured underfoot.

forebody. The front section of the ski or the area ahead of the waist.

forerunners. Skiers who set up slalom courses and test the conditions before a race.

freestyle. An acrobatic type of skiing that includes the disciplines of ballet, moguls, and aerials.

friction. The resistance formed by the ski's sliding on the snow. This friction actually melts snow under a ski's base, creating a thin layer of water.

front-entry boot. A type of ski boot with outer-shell hinges that open at the front.

front pole flip. A ballet move in which the skier turns a somersault over his or her poles.

frostbite. A dangerous medical condition in which the cell tissue of body extremities freezes when exposed to the elements.

gaper. Someone who pauses to take in the beautiful scenery at the top of a slope.

gate. A set of flags or poles through which racers ski.

giant slalom. A race that tests high-speed turning ability.

gondola. A type of enclosed ski lift usually reserved for long transport distances. Can accommodate from two to ten passengers.

gravity. The force that pulls an object closer to the earth or a skier down a mountain.

green circles. The designation for a beginner slope, marked on ski resort trail maps and signage.

groomed. Trails that have been smoothed out after a storm or a previous ski day.

hardpack. A hard, compacted surface.

heli-skiing. Natural off-trail skiing accessed by helicopter.

hinge-point. The flex point of the boot, where it hinges forward.

hotdogging. Freestyle mogul skiing.

hourglass. A revolutionary type of ski, especially recommended for beginners and intermediates because of its easy-to-turn hourglass design or exaggerated sidecut.

hypothermia. A dangerous situation that occurs when one's core body temperature is reduced as a result of exposure to extreme cold.

inner boot. The removable interior lining of a ski boot, designed for support, warmth, and comfort.

intermediate. Skiing ability level between beginner and advanced or expert.

intermediate run. A trail of moderate difficulty, usually marked on map and signage by a blue square.

intermediate ski. A model that's versatile, easy to turn, and more tolerant of speed than a beginner ski.

inverted aerial. A midair, freestyle somersault.

J-bar. A surface lift with J-shaped bars that pull skiers uphill.

jump. Nordic event that involves descending from a ramp and sailing off a launch.

lift. Any of a variety of mechanisms used to transport skiers uphill.

lift line. The line formed as people organize to load onto a lift, usually marked by ropes.

lift tickets. Tickets, often laminated and/or attached with hooks, that act as a skier's pass to the ski area and its lifts for a specified period of time.

loading. The act of getting onto a lift.

mashed potatoes. Wet, heavy snow.

mid-entry boot. A hybrid design that hinges open at the middle of the shell. Offers support similar to that of front-entry boots, with improved entry convenience.

moguls. From the Alps colloquialism *mugel*, which means "small mound." These bumps are formed when skiers repeatedly turn along the same path.

mogul field. A slope covered with moguls.

mogul skiing. A freestyle form of competitive skiing in which skiers race down mogul fields.

never-ever. A first-time skier.

Nordic. *See* **cross-country skiing**.

off-trail (also **off-piste**). An ungroomed, unpatrolled slope not usually part of an established ski area.

packed powder. Snow that has been groomed into a firm, compacted surface.

point. The pointed end tip of a ski pole at the opposite end from the handle.

pole. A balancing and timing stick with a grip on one end and a basket on the other.

poling. The act of planting ski poles in the snow during a ski turn to facilitate the turn.

poma. A surface lift that pulls skiers uphill with bars that have disks attached. The disks are placed between the legs, against the buttocks.

powder. Light, dry, fresh snow.

rear-entry boot. A type of ski boot with shell hinges that open at the back. This is, generally, the most comfortable type of boot and the easiest to put on.

rope tow. The simplest surface lift in which a long, revolving loop of rope pulls skiers uphill.

running surface. The polished underside or base of the ski.

schussing. Skiing straight downhill, often in a full tuck position, with skis close together.

shell. The hard outer ski boot, most often made of plastic, with a hinged opening for foot entry.

shovel or **tip.** The front of the ski that curves upward.

sidecut. The hourglass shape of a ski that allows the ski, when pressured, to carve a turn.

ski alpining. Touring mountain terrain on skis, to include both ascending and descending mountains.

ski brake. Hinged arms, part of the binding's heel piece, that swing down and stop the ski when the boot and binding separate in a fall.

skidding. When a ski slides through a turn instead of carving a smooth arc.

Ski Code. Internationally recognized rules of skiing courtesy and etiquette.

ski jumping (also **ski flying**). A competition in which skiers launch themselves off large ramps and land as far as possible downhill.

ski mountaineering. *See* **ski alpining**.

Ski Patrol. Specially trained experts who act as police, rescue, and first-aid personnel at a ski resort.

ski simulators. Mechanical devices that allow the user to simulate various skiing actions.

slalom. A race in which a skier must maneuver quickly and efficiently between a series of closely spaced gates on a course.

sliding (also **flat-running**). When a ski glides over the snow with no edging applied.

snowboard. A single wide board on which a rider straps his feet and slides down the slope in much the same way a surfer rides a wave.

snowboarding. An exciting, growing sport that combines the elements of surfing, skateboarding, and skiing.

snowplow. A high-friction technique taught to beginning skiers for balance and control.

steering. The act of guiding the ski through a turn with subtle motions of the feet.

super-G (super giant slalom). A race that combines the turning technique of a giant slalom with the speed of downhill.

T-bar. A type of surface lift that pulls the skier uphill via a T-shaped bar.

tail. The rear of a ski.

telemark skiing. A type of downhill skiing performed on thinner, cross-country-like skis with a modified binding that allows heel attachment.

tilting. The rolling of skis onto their edges.(*see* also **edging**)

tip. The very front end of the ski, always curved upward.

tow-lifts. Mechanical devices that tow, or lift, skiers up the slope.

trail. A well-marked, well-patrolled, and carefully maintained ski run.

trail map. A map showing the layout of a ski area's trails and their levels of difficulty.

tram. Large enclosed cabins or trolleys, suspended from cables, that transport dozens of skiers at a time up the hill, usually to the mountaintop.

tree line. The altitude at which trees stop growing.

tuck. A low crouch that provides the most aerodynamic body position for fast downhill skiing.

turn. Any motion where the skis change direction.

ungroomed. Trails that have been left untouched after a storm or a previous ski day.

unloading. The act of getting off a lift at the top of the mountain.

waist. The central portion of the ski where the binding is found.

water aerobics. Calisthenics-type exercises performed in a swimming pool. These exercises enhance endurance and cardiovascular strength, as well as train the body to conform to restrictive elements.

whiteout. Zero-visibility conditions experienced in a heavy snowstorm.

wicking. A characteristic of ski clothing design that moves moisture away from the surface of the skin.

wind-chill factor. A calculation of how cold the air feels, based on a combination of temperature and wind speed.

yard sale. A wipeout fall in which skis, poles, goggles, hat, and other belongings end up strewn along the mountainside.

yoga. Popular method of exercise that builds strength and flexibility while focusing one's powers of concentration.